I0663417

Captured Lightning

Award-Winning Student Articles
Volume I

Captured Lightning

Award-Winning Student MagazineArticles

• Volume I •

edited by
Ann deG Marshall and Alison J. Wright

apprentice
house

Baltimore, Maryland
www.apprenticehouse.com

Edited by Ann deG Marshall and Alison J. Wright

Cover and internal design by
Ann deG Marshall and Alison J. Wright

First printing
10 9 8 7 6 5 4 3 2 1

ISBN: 1-934074-07-1
ISBN 13-Digit: 978-1-934074-07-7

apprentice
house

Baltimore, Maryland
www.apprenticehouse.com

"The difference between the right word and the almost right word is the difference between lightning and a lightning bug."
-Mark Twain

Captured Lightning is the first of what we hope to be an annual publication of AEJMC award-winning magazine articles written by college students across the country. Apprentice House, as a student-run organization, is proud and pleased to publish the award-winning works of our peers.

AEJMC, the Association for Education in Journalism and Mass Communication, continues to set the highest standards for student work. Their annual magazine writing contest highlights the outstanding work of journalism students throughout the country – and 2005 was no exception. The students represented in this compilation certainly meet, if not exceed, the AEJMC level of excellence, with topics ranging from drag shows to awareness of AIDS in Africa.

As a non profit, student-staffed publishing house organized by the Communication Department at Loyola College in Maryland, Apprentice House approached this project with enthusiasm. Having worked closely for the past months with professors, advisors and, most significantly, student writers to produce such an outstanding compilation of work, has been a powerful reminder of what can be accomplished with hard work and determination – no matter what one's age or level of experience.

As college seniors, our work on Captured Lightning has been frustrating, fun, challenging and fulfilling – much like our college careers. On that note, we look forward confidently and expectantly to a long tradition of team-work between student writers and student publishers in the continuing pursuit of capturing creative lightning.

Enjoy!

Ann Marshall
Alison Wright

Loyola College in Maryland

contents

consumer magazine article: service & information

consumer magazine article: first person

specialized business press article

Consumer Magazine Article: Places

billy goat gruff goes to washington

Sarah Bailey, Northwestern University

The city of donkeys and elephants is about to have a goat.

It's not just any goat that's coming to Washington, D.C. It's the Goat – as Chicago's Billy Goat Tavern is known on its home turf. In August, the Goat's owner, Sam Sianis, plans to open a new branch of his populist bar in the nation's capital.

With its epithet-hurling Greek servers, red-and-white checked tablecloths, and an eight-item menu topped by a $4.35 double cheeseburger, the Goat has become a Chicago landmark. Its earthy ambiance has attracted enough journalists and celebrities to impress the most shameless Washington name dropper. The Goat has political panache, too: Politicans from President Bush to Hillary Clinton have dropped by in the last 15 years. But it remains to be seen how a place straight out of the movie My Big Fat Greek Wedding will play amid the expense-account swollen watering holes of Capitol Hill.

It was the National Association of Realtors that persuaded Sam Sianis to send a delegate to Washington. The trade group owns the Michigan Avenue building above the place the Goat calls home. When the realtors decided to open a Washington office, they quickly realized they could not leave home without their Goat. So the group proposed that the restaurant come along. Sianis hesitated at first. "The family's had this bar for 70 years now and it's never left Chicago," his eldest son Billy says. "But after we talked for a long time we decided, 'Hey, let's try something new.'"

Cheezeborger! Cheezeborger!

When the Sianises move this summer, they are not sure what type of crowd their new location will attract. There are 878,000 different restaurants nationally, and four out of five new restaurants fail within their first year, according to the National Restaurant Association. In order to compete, each must have a special quality. The Goat's name has cachet. But will the restaurant's mystique as a Chicago place survive in D.C?

After all, the Goat has been a unique windy city institution since it first opened in 1934. Founder Gus Sianis created the place as a hangout where locals could get cheap food and drinks during the Depression. But it was Chicago's writers who made the bar special. Located just a stone's throw from the Chicago Tribune offices, journalists quickly made it into a late-night second home. Then they wrote about it so much it finally became a Chicago icon. When Mike Kilian was a 22-year-old rookie reporter at the Tribune, for example, he would finish up his stories around midnight. Then, ready to relax, he and his cohorts would descend from the snowy white Tribune tower and make their way towards the neon sign of relief peeping out from the looming shadows of the Grand Street Bridge, the sign that signaled the singular comforts of the tavern.

Three groups went to the Goat after deadline: the pressmen, young reporters and the famous Tribune columnist Mike Royko – a group of one, Kilian notes. It was always rowdy late night. Royko made the restaurant the setting for so many of his columns that Chicago readers felt it was their own neighborhood bar. The tavern is devoted to its journalist patrons. Framed pictures and articles by such writers as CBS anchor Walter Cronkite and movie critic Roger Ebert hang on each wall.

But journalists are in short supply around the Goat these days. Some loyalists, such as Tribune columnists Rick Kogan and John Kass, still frequent the bar by day – Kass eats an egg sandwich and reads the newspaper there every morning at 10:00 am. But the restaurant has overflowed with tourists ever since 1977 when John Belushi brought the bar national attention with his "Saturday Night Live" routine – mimicking the Goat's Greek servers yelling, "Cheezeborger! Cheezborger! No fries – chips!" Since then tourists have swarmed the place – at least three bus loads crowd in on Saturdays. As a result fewer journalists and locals think of it as their secret escape.

Goat in the Political Zoo

Tourists may scare off journalists, but they help the Goat financially. In the last two decades the restaurant has begun dishing up its famous burgers in three other Chicago locations. Now the Goat will try Washington, but some wonder how successful a Goat can be in such a political city.

The bar has a forthright quality that may confuse a city immersed in politics. During the 1944 Republican Convention, William "Billy Goat" Sianis put a sign on his door that read: "No Republicans Allowed." The phrase had a magnetic attraction. Soon GOP stalwarts were swarming the bar demanding service. In 1991, then President George H. W. Bush rearranged a day of meetings in Chicago to make a surprise appearance at the Goat. He wanted to meet Royko, then the city's best-known columnist. But Royko – never one to bow to VIPs – responded he would rather watch the William Kennedy Smith rape trial on T.V. Sianis framed Royko's column about that incident and hung it, together with three from other columnists express-ing outrage at the Bush visit – on the tavern's left wall.

Though the bar is primarily Democratic, the Goat's regular patrons did not exactly roll out the red carpet for Sen. Hillary Rodham Clinton [D-NY], either. In 2001 the Senator took the unprecedented step of renting the entire place for a night meeting. The Secret Service required the Sianises to lock the doors and plan an escape route in case of an emergency. The Goat's regulars were furious. They threw food at the locked doors and shouted in protest, demanding their regular spots at the bar. Such loyal objections could be expected in a city that hosted the 1968 riots, but the behavior wouldn't be acceptable in an area of conference calls and lobbyists.

D.C. Crossover

Marketing would be a drastic change for an establishment that prides itself on never advertising, so Sam Sianis will avoid promotions. Since friends first started raving about the bar in the 1930s, the place has thrived on reputation alone. "My dad has never advertised," says son Tom Sianis. With reporters writing columns about the bar frequently, the Goat has always had all the free publicity it needed. "He has never once asked someone to write a story, that's why people do it," Tom Sianis adds.

Sianis says the Goat has "tons of friends" – former Chicagoans now living in Washington who will try to help the bar remain ad free. The family has started calling members of this clan to ask them to spread the word that the new Goat is opening. Many former Tribune reporters have moved on to the Washington Post or D.C. bureaus of other papers, bringing die-hard Goat loyalties with them. Chicago politicians love the Goat, too, so the Sianises figure they have a wide base of support.

But Kilian says that touristy restaurants in Washington,

such as Planet Hollywood, have failed recently because big names alone aren't enough to pull in big crowds. "This is a pinstripe and briefcase type of town filled with people who go home to the suburbs at night – not to bars," Kilian says.

Pinstriped politicos would indeed be new for a restaurant used to serving customers in jeans and t-shirts. Anthony Greco, a journalism graduate student in Northwestern University's Washington program, says he thinks it would be hard for the Goat to replace the National Press Club as a hangout for journalists. Greco, 24, represents the twenty-something journalism audience that used to flood the Goat. But Greco said that right now he and his friends never go out during the week. They conduct interviews and cover congressional hearings and political meetings during the day, so by 6:00 pm they are usually exhausted. They usually rent a movie and go home. On Thursday and Friday nights they may stroll half a block to the National Press Club and enjoy student drink specials, but they wouldn't catch a cab over to the Goat. "The Press Club is where most journalism action is in Washington," Greco says. "There's always something going on. I can't really see the Goat replacing that."

Steve Rhodes, editor of Chicago Magazine thinks writers just party less nowadays. "Younger journalists are so lame right now anyway that they're probably going to Starbucks instead of a bar after work," Rhodes says. "Maybe the Goat just needs to make some changes. They don't even have music playing in there right now. What kind-of newspaper bar doesn't have great rock and roll?"

The food selection may fail to attract customers too. In Washington, the Goat will add an open "beer garden" outside where people can drink and eat. But the eight item menu will stay the same, and so will the prices. A triple cheeseburger will still sell for under $5. "The Goat was popular in my day with people looking for cheap eats and drinks," said Kilian, who now works as a Tribune Washington correspondent. "I don't know if you'll find people wanting that in Washington. This is really a salad kind of place."

Greco says that even twenty-somethings don't like burgers in Washington like they do in Chicago. "All of my friends just want to go grab a salad at lunch, myself included," Greco adds. He explains he couldn't "eat burgers as greasy as the Goat's every day and still live very long."

The Sianises will also keep Chicago journalism as the bar's theme. Billy Sianis explains that they plan to still hang framed Chicago newspaper clips as wall decorations. But after the opening they may add some articles from Washington journalists. "We'll see how things go, but if we can get some good Post columns or clips we may start hanging those too." Billy said. "We're not completely sure what direction we're taking this place yet."

Kilian thinks that keeping a strictly Chicago theme will be good for the bar. "I think they need to keep a Chicago flavor because otherwise they're not themselves, and that's not what people want," he said. "People will like having a little bit of a real city here. I don't think Washington is a real city. It's a federal park with some parasitical buildings around it for lawyers and lobbyists. A Chicago bar would attract the large number of people here who came from Chicago and miss it."

The Sianises are also looking for Greeks who can work in the Washington location. Many people flock to the Goat just to hear servers like Tom Sakkos, a Greek man who has worked at the Goat for 14 years, yelling at people when they walk in: "Come in, sit down, get a double burger! No da triple is beder! Get da triple!" He claims nine out of 10 people always order the double, but he keeps pushing for the triple with every person anyway. In order for the new Goat to be successful, the workers need to yell with the same vigor as the current ones. So Sianis is combing the Washington area searching for Greeks with vigorous lungs. "He'll probably start looking around at the local penitentiary," Tom Sianis jokes. "He needs to find tough waiters." Once Sianis finds potential waiters, he will transport some of his current servers to Washington to teach the news ones the tricks of the trade. Greco says the Greeks' yelling style might intimidate some people on the Hill when they first walk into the bar. "I wonder if people will realize that they're kidding around when they yell at you right away," Greco says. "People around here can be kinda stiff. That could scare some of them off."

Also, in order to keep track of the new place, the Sianises have to break down and buy their first computers. "My dad works non-stop right now, going from bar to bar, manually keeping track of sales and everything else," Billy Sianis says. The family does still plan on keeping the Chicago Goat computer free, but Billy Sianis says they may upgrade their cash register; they currently use the same one they've had since the Goat opened its Michigan Avenue location in 1964.

Chicago in a bottle

With long-standing traditions and unchanged technology, it figures that some people are angry that the Sianises are moving a Chicago bulwark. "To me, the move kind-of detracts from the Billy Goat mystique of a special Chicago place," Rhodes says. "It hypes the brand name and gives people a reason to not have overly romantic feelings about the place. You can't bottle bar magic and try to export it."

Killian is also skeptical about whether the Goat will survive in a place that's "not even a real city." He added: "There are few things that were as unique as the BG. It belongs in a tough town. People in Washington are workaholics. Parties are work. You can't bring a bar like the Billy Goat to a place like that."

Rhodes worries about the politicians: "It will attract tourists and politicians, but is that what you really want? Do you want Trent Lott drinking in your bar? No, you want Trent Lott as far away from your bar as possible."

Congressmen may order burgers at the Goat. The skeptics could be right and the Goat will fail. Or perhaps the bar will help add a little night life and relax one of the nation's most uppity cities.

But this summer the Sianises will see if their simple Goat will find friends among a stubborn jackass and a slow-moving elephant and break loose in Washington's political zoo.

notes from underground
Robert Perkins, University of Kansas

The door opens a crack immediately after I knock on it. From inside the house, a figure lurking in the shadows peers out at me.

"Hello?" the figure asks.

"Um, this might sound like a weird question, but is this where the Haunted Kitchen is?" I ask. I know full well that it is, but I don't want to alarm my barely visible host by making any accusations.

"Just a second." The figure leaves the cracked doorway to consult with someone behind the door. It is early in the afternoon on a Wednesday and I'm hoping to talk to the guys responsible for the Haunted Kitchen, one of Lawrence's underground music venues. The Kitchen is run out of the house that I'm standing in front of, whose address the owners have asked me not to publish. The guys in charge have a reputation for being secretive, which has helped them avoid the trouble with the law that other, similar venues face.

From behind the door I hear a barely audible "... wants to know about the Haunted Kitchen," followed by a murmured response. Just as my eyes begin to adjust to the darkness behind the sliver of doorway that I'm peering into, the door swings open and two guys with long hair and black t-shirts invite me inside.

As it turns out, I'm face-to-face with Jeff Milner and Daniel Noakes, the guys who do most of the work for the Haunted Kitchen. When they're not at their day jobs or practicing with their band, the two spend their time booking bands and setting up shows.

They've been friends since they were kids together back

in Oklahoma City, and have been running music venues for the better part of a decade, yet they're both only 22 now.

When we met later for an interview, I discovered that I had stumbled upon a world unto itself, a world I hadn't even imagined existed. I'd stumbled onto DIY. DIY, which stands for Do It Yourself, is an anti-consumerism counterculture that exists not only in music but in film, art, and anything else that people have gotten fed up with buying from corporations and want to make for themselves. DIY music venues are pieced together by music lovers who build stages in their basements, build or buy their own sound equipment and host their own shows – usually free of charge, as they tend to exist in areas that aren't zoned for commercial activity. On Saturday, Feb. 19, I set out to experience the world of DIY by hitting as many underground shows as I could in one night, starting with the Haunted Kitchen.

The Haunted Kitchen is really the basement of a decrepit old house near the student ghetto. The first thing you notice when you see it – after the flaking yellow paint – is the porch, which looks precariously like the deck of a sinking ship. Somehow it manages to support a stained couch by the front door, where a half dozen people hang out to smoke while the show's going on. I get there painfully early, so the porch is empty when I arrive. The flier had said that the show began at 8 p.m., which actually means 11 as it turns out.

Inside, old couches held down by silent, half-awake guys wearing black hoodies make up the bulk of the living room's furniture, along with a hefty stereo system on the wall blasting a hardcore punk CD when I get there. While the house's tenants tend to be into punk and metal, they say that they've booked all kinds of bands, including local indie rock groups.

The Kitchen's décor matches the musical tastes of its occupants. Posters from a couple of bands and random artwork, some of it Noakes', patchily cover the walls. Beyond the kitchen at the back of the house lies the door to the real Kitchen – the basement. As small as it is, the basement is impressively well laid-out. Milner and Noakes have been doing DIY shows since they were 15, so they full well know how to set up a basement venue. When they first got the house, it already had a short stage built in the corner. They added a merchandise bar in the adjacent corner and a slew of decorations, like a plastic head hanging from the ceiling by a hook. Pillows sit in all of the window cases with foam eggcrate scattered around on the walls to muffle sound to the outside. They say that their neighbors never complain about the noise, and that the only time they had any real trouble with the police was when someone accidentally left the back door open, which they now keep locked shut.

The basement holds about 30 or so people, though when I get there – way too early – there are only a couple of people milling around. Noakes is the first to greet me as I walk inside, offering me a beer and the spot where he'd been sitting on the broken futon against the living room wall. He apologizes for the quality of the beer (Milwaukee's Best) as he presses the warm can into my hand, reminding me for all the world of my parents apologizing to company about the quality of their food whenever guests arrive for a dinner party. He frets a little about the lack of people at first, but he doesn't need to worry – about 40 more people will show up before the show starts. Though the Kitchen relies entirely on word-of-mouth and fliers to advertise, their shows tend to draw enough people to fill the basement.

As the night wears on, I find myself talking to an

orange-haired girl who is a bit tipsy from pre-partying and a diminutive-looking guy who seems to know everyone in the house. The girl is a freshman at the University of Kansas, and both are veterans of Lawrence DIY shows.

"I just have to see the Roustabouts," the girl gushes, talking about the headlining band. She turns to address the other guy, whom she knows from before. "Did you see them last time they came through?" He laughs.

"Uh, sort of. I was on mushrooms at the time, and I kind of freaked out and had to leave." Eventually the two leave me to go have a smoke on the porch, so I join a couple of other guys in helping the Roustabouts to carry in their equipment. The guys in the Roustabouts tell me that though they don't play a lot of DIY shows (they're still in high school, which makes touring difficult), they know Noakes and Milner from the old days when the two used to run DIY venues back in Oklahoma City and have come up specifically to see them. Some bands, however, tour the DIY circuit almost exclusively. Milner and Noakes say they've brought in bands from as far away as the Netherlands, which is amazing considering that the bands don't really get paid.

The money issue is a big one for DIY venues. As it would be illegal for residents of a house to charge money for holding shows in their basements – the houses are in residential, not commercial, zones – the people running DIY venues almost always ask for donations to pay for the band's gas and such. The line between 'donation' and 'entry fee' can be a thin one for police wanting to shut down a continual noise problem or landlords wanting to protect their property from the damage that is associated with running a DIY venue. Meredith Vacek, who graduated from the University last May, used to live at the Pink House and now lives at the Horror House, and says that a misunderstanding about money was one of the things that got her first venue shut down. She and her former roommates at the Pink House used to run shows in their living room until a couple of articles published in the Lawrence Journal-World reported that, among other things, the Pink House was charging admission. Pete Berard, who also used to live there, says that he and his roommates did shows only as a "labor of love," but that the landlord shut the venue down shortly after the articles ran. Berard, who graduated in December, moved out to New York last month to continue his labor of love by working for Domino Records, Franz Ferdinand's label.

The Pink House was just one of the DIY venues to pop up in Lawrence during the past five years. Seniors at the University of Kansas might also remember shows at the Halfway House, the Pirate House, the Horror House and the Kremlin. The residents of these houses formed a network for underground music in Lawrence. They all knew each other; the residents of the Pink House and Halfway House in particular used to hang out together all the time, and they both used the same guy as the Pirate House to book bands sometimes. And almost every member of each house has been involved with KJHK at some point during their time in Lawrence. Yet despite their closeness, the houses booked a wide variety of music. Vacek says that while the Pirate House focused on punk and crust metal, the Halfway House and Pink House pulled in all kinds of bands: punk, pop, screamo, avante garde post punk – you name it. Neil Mulka, Leavenworth senior and former resident of the Kremlin, says that his house would take in whoever was willing to play there. With DIY venues, availability of bands often determines a show's content more than the musical tastes of the house's residents.

At about 11 the opening band, Öroku, goes on. Öroku is the Haunted Kitchen's house band. All five of the members live in the house; Milner is the lead singer and Noakes plays guitar. As soon as they assemble on the stage, the incandescent lights are replaced with red ones and the collection of long-haired, black-wearing guys rip into a set of crust metal songs for an audience of about 20 people. The environment is as relaxed as the music is loud. Dylan Desmond, a former resident of the Pirate House, happens to be in the crowd that night. Desmond, Overland Park, senior, lived at the Pirate House for a year when it was still a DIY venue. He says he still tries to hit DIY shows every now and then. The community was and is tight, which is why it wasn't surprising to find out that the guys from 1331 Vermont – my next stop for the evening – know all about the Haunted Kitchen and had even been to a couple of shows there.

The only thing the Haunted Kitchen and 1331 Vermont have in common, aside from both being DIY venues, is that they're both yellow houses. While the Kitchen is the very embodiment of secrecy and organization, 1331 Vermont has an open, haphazard feel to it. It doesn't even have a name; it's just "1331 Vermont." And while Milner and Noakes of the Haunted Kitchen have asked me not to publish their address, the residents of the other yellow house were more than happy to see their address in the paper, saying that they hope it will attract more people to their shows. Despite the lack of an address on the outside of the house, I have no problem finding it. Loud music blasts from the door as a swarm of people spill out of it, covering the porch and the lawn. With a crowd of easily 60 people milling about holding plastic cups, it lookes more like a house party than anything else, which is roughly what the residents are going for. Patrick Struebing and Kevin Thompson, two of the four people who live at 1331 Vermont, say that the events at their house aren't strictly shows or parties, but more a combination of the two.

In a tiny living room sandwiched between the kitchen, filled with kegs, and the foyer, filled with people looking for kegs, is Ike Turner Overdrive and at least 30 cheering people. I elbow my way around, trying to find a good spot, but eventually give up and resign myself to getting bumped into continuously by the stream of keg traffic. As I stand there, mashed in a crowd of people wearing hipster clothes and thick black-rimmed glasses, the lead singer and guitarist of Ike Turner Overdrive rip their shirts off and decide to deafen me with driving, high-energy rock. Thompson says that he and his roommates don't have a specific musical preference for the bands they book; they usually just ask their friends' bands to play their shows. In this case, at least, they seem to have lucked out and to have been friends with a band that the crowd likes. The audience screams and cheers at the end of every song, completely unlike the relaxed, Zen-like enjoyment of Öroku at the Haunted Kitchen. Near the end of Ike Turner Overdrive's set, the guitarist starts spraying whatever he was drinking over the crowd, nailing us at point-blank range.

Patrick and Kevin say that 1331 Vermont tends to have some crazy party/shows, which can be expensive for them. The night that I went to see them, Kevin got a $70 ticket from the police because of a noise complaint from an unknown neighbor – unknown thanks to the new Lawrence code that allows people to make such complaints anonymously. While the Haunted Kitchen has homemade soundproofing to prevent problems like that, 1331 Vermont has a broken window that does nothing to stop the music from leaking out. They also had a bathroom door kicked down by a member of the band Vibralux, who claimed he thought there was an orgy going on inside. Add that to the lovely pencil mural of random people's outlined faces found on their wall that they'll have to explain to their landlord, and all of the personal belongings that always get stolen from any DIY venue, and you can see that they aren't making any money on this deal. But when I asked if they were going to stop having shows because of the expenses (particularly the ticket), I got a laugh and a "fuck that – no" from Kevin. "We're having a party five days after I have to pay the fine." he says. Patrick says that they keep on hosting events because, after years of going to great parties in Lawrence, he and his roommates want to give something back to the community. That, and they just really like to have huge parties.

The last venue I want to hit is Solidarity, at 1119 Massachusetts. After parking my car, I walk past the Greek-looking crowd outside of It's Brothers and find my way to the radical library. There's no music – the first bad sign. The lights are off; also bad. Finally I see a sign on the door that says the show had been cancelled. Later I was told that the show had been cancelled because the band had broken up – no guarantees in DIY, but then, even mainstream venues are subject to cancellations.

Solidarity does double duty as both a radical library and a music venue. Volunteers Kat Randolph and Katy Andrus say that the venue does about two shows each month, packing people into the deceptively large space. Originally, they were worried that they'd have problems with the police (being right across from the station), but Randolph and Andrus say that It's Brothers and the dance studio next door tend to make much more noise. One of the driving forces behind the music at Solidarity is Dave Strano, who has lived at the Pirate House (well, former Pirate House – now its tenants call it the Joe Hill House) since the days when it was still a music venue.

The main way that the DIY scene actually works is simply word-of-mouth, friend-to-friend communication, says Vacek of the former Pink House. With her punky hair and multiple piercings, Vacek sticks out in the typical Lawrence crowd, and she seems to know everyone. She says that she and her roommates never had trouble finding enough people to fill their house for shows. When it comes to organizing on a national scale, DIY venues and the bands that play at them turn to a higher power: Book Your Own Fuckin' Life. BYOFL began its life as a page in the Maximumrocknroll Magazine 15 years ago. Venues, bands and anyone who had a couch for traveling punk musicians to crash on posted their contact information. The page quickly became an independent book, which came out once each year. The problem with this was the considerable cost of putting out such a publication – sans advertising, which would be counter to the generally anti-consumerism bent of the DIY scene – made it expensive to produce. In addition, the original editors grew frustrated that much of the information would be outdated by the time it made its yearly run. Eventually the book went on the Internet at www.byofl.org. Today it's run by Ernst Schoen-Rene, a self-described "computer guy" who took over after a devastating computer crash that wiped out a lot of information three years ago. It has 17,000 listings for bands, venues, labels, promoters, etc. and gets 15,000 hits every day. Schoen-Rene also runs New Disorder Records and used to play in the punk band Jack Acid, which worked the DIY circuit from '91 to '92. In Lawrence, the Haunted Kitchen is listed on the site, but the guys from 1331 Vermont haven't even heard of it and the volunteers from Solidarity say they should really get around to listing themselves on it one of these days.

Schoen-Rene says that the DIY scene started about 25 years ago, mostly as a result of how small and connected the punk rock community was. People would pass around lists of who to call to find a venue or a couch to crash on. As no one back then got into punk rock to make money – this was before the days when bands like Blink 182 made punk rock into pop – everyone was more or less in it for the love of the music, Schoen-Rene says. During those early years, there were venues a-plenty and tons of donation money. Bands could pay for all of the gas and food and make a little on the side too, Schoen-Rene says. Now, he says, the money's tighter and a lot of the bands are in it with a delusion of making it big. The golden years are over, he says.

The scene is far from dead, however. BYOFL is still going strong and Bruce Haring, founder of the DIY Convention, says it's only continuing to grow. The DIY Convention started in 2000 and drew more than 1,000 people this year. Haring says that with the rise of digital tools like the Internet, DIY has gotten huge – for better or for worse. "You have a ton of people producing out there now, which means you get a lot of really great stuff and a lot of shit," he says. Also, DIY has branched out from punk to other genres, to an extent changing the types of people associated with the scene.

Locally, despite the loss of venues like the Pink House, the Pirate House and the Kremlin, there are still places like the Haunted Kitchen, 1331 Vermont and Solidarity that plan to keep having shows. In addition, ex-Kremlin resident Emily Elmore says she is planning to start a new DIY venue with her friend April Flemming and anyone else they decide to live with. The Springfield, Mo., senior says that she and Flemming are hoping to find a place in the student ghetto – a welcome change for Elmore, who moved to Eudora after leaving the Kremlin – and plan to start having shows as early as this May.

I drive past the Haunted Kitchen on my way home. My route doesn't take me by 1331 Vermont, but if it had I probably would have seen the police handing them their $70 ticket while the party raged on. Instead, I see a quiet crowd smoking on the porch – probably unaware of all of the work that has gone into the evening they're enjoying – just waiting for the next band to go on.

Consumer Magazine Article: People

teeth in the closet: an odyssey of abuse

Christopher Sheppard, Arizona State University

Bob, a 56-year-old unemployed construction worker, fired up his Harley Davidson outside the Iron Horse Saloon in North Phoenix. He was of medium height and build. His thinning brown hair hung in a mop on his head. His blue eyes wandered down the street and lazily scanned for oncoming traffic. He felt good. His buzz gave him courage.

"Let's go get some wings!" he yelled to his friends Tom and Drew.

His friends rolled out of the parking lot ahead of him, their Harleys belching a throaty snarl. His only thought as he roared onto the street was looking cool. He accelerated wildly, laying a rooster tail of sparks as the Harley's tail pipes scraped the asphalt. Bob barely kept the bike under control as he turned and rocketed down the street. His only thought now was getting to Hooters quickly for some wings and more beer.

"Oh, God, I'm sorry about this, Jenny," Pamela said to her friend as she shook her head. Pamela, Bob's wife, was utterly embarrassed. Pamela was also of medium height and build, with dyed red hair and brown eyes. Her weathered face spoke of many hard, stressful years. Also 56, she could only shake her head in disgust that her husband was acting like a 19-year-old in front of her long-time friends.

Pamela got into the car with Jenny and Becky. They had come all the way from Indiana to visit her, only to watch Bob drink himself stupid. As they headed to Hooters, she wished the night would be mercifully short.

Bob consumed three more beers at Hooters. He was overly amorous with Pamela, and she didn't know how to take it. Bob had long ago ceased to show interest in her. The public displays of affection, at Hooters no less, were disconcerting to her.

When the women got back to Bob and Pamela's house, the three men on their hogs were already in the driveway. Pamela hit the garage door opener. Bob saw the garage door opening up and decided to look cool again. He gunned the Harley, and it bolted toward the garage while the door was only two-thirds of the way up. Bob missed hitting his unprotected head by a fraction of an inch.

Bob barreled into the garage and crashed headlong into a stack of souvenirs and gifts Jenny and Becky had bought earlier in the week. Bob killed the bike and looked around. Broken gifts and souvenirs lay all over the garage. He began to stammer broken apologies to Jenny and Becky. The women just looked at each other and decided this was the end of the evening. Jenny and Becky awkwardly wished Pamela a good night, got into the car, and drove to their hotel.

Bob went into the house for another beer.

Pamela sighed. She was tired and embarrassed.

Pamela didn't realize she was about to become a domestic violence statistic. She didn't understand that the night's events would cause her to become a refugee from her own life. Pamela couldn't comprehend that she would endure a year of physical, mental, emotional, and legal suffering.

She closed the garage door and wearily entered the house.

This Doesn't Develop in One Night

Pamela and Bob had been married 20 years earlier. They clicked from the start. They had found a relationship where each could talk to the other about anything. Pamela was more comfortable with Bob than with any man she'd ever met.

About five years ago, their relationship began to erode. Bob slipped from being merely a heavy drinker into alcoholism. So slowly, in fact, that Pamela dismissed each new warning sign as a coincidence or bad luck.

Around 1998, Bob started drinking heavily. He had torn his rotator cuff in a snowmobile accident while drinking. He couldn't work, so he filled his newfound free time with beer.

Bob's best friend, Tom, found Bob a job supervising a roofing crew. Tom also enabled Bob to pursue his beer-drinking hobby on the job. They were very discrete about drinking and roofing.

Tom eventually lost his business because of a construction-related mishap. Bob was unemployed again. Tom managed to work out a deal where both he and Bob would go work for another company. Both men continued to sip beer while working until the company office began receiving calls from customers complaining that they could smell alcohol on their breath. Bob was "laid off" in early 2002. In reality, he was fired because of drinking on the job.

Now collecting unemployment, Bob could devote more time to his drinking hobby. His friends would come over during the day and at night. Bob never got hammered; he just maintained a steady buzz with a coozie-covered beer in his hand.

Bob began mistreating Pamela early in 2002. Since he wasn't working, Pamela assumed responsibility for the family finances. She worked 40 hours a week as a dispatcher for a steel company, but the money wasn't enough to make ends meet. When money became tight, Bob would verbally abuse Pamela. He would become irate, screaming at her and blaming her for the family's financial difficulties.

Bob and Pamela didn't celebrate Christmas in 2002 because their bank account was empty. Even though they couldn't afford to buy presents for Bob's three children (from a previous marriage), he always managed to find money in their joint checking account to keep the refrigerator stocked with beer.

The financial stress and Bob's verbal abuse eventually took their toll on Pamela. Early in January 2003, her body failed her.

In January, Pamela came home from work to find Bob trying to set up an office in one of the spare rooms. He wanted to start a roofing company and said he needed her help to move furniture into the new office.

"Bob, I'm tired and don't want to do this tonight," Pamela said.

Bob looked crestfallen, then angry. He snarled, "You never want to help me get ahead. You don't care if my business succeeds, do you? I can't believe you are so selfish!"

Pamela acquiesced and helped Bob even though she was dog-tired and not feeling well. She figured it was better to do what he wanted than be subjected to a guilt trip all night. After they were done, Pamela went to bed, exhausted.

She woke up in the middle of the night with a strange feeling in her arms, chest, and stomach. There was no pain, just a sensation she had never experienced before. Pamela called 911. The fire department showed up quickly and took her to the hospital.

The doctors told Pamela she had had a mild heart attack. As she lay in the emergency room, the doctors recommended an angioplasty. Scared, she agreed, and the doctors anesthetized her. When she awoke, she was told she had just undergone a double bypass. The doctors had harvested veins for the bypass from her right leg. She looked down to find her breastbone stapled up and stitches down her chest and all over her legs.

Pamela went back to work one month after open-heart surgery. Bob wasn't working, and they were in dire financial straits. Someone had to pay the bills. On February 18, only three days after she returned to work, her leg became infected. The pain was excruciating. She spent another week in the hospital on antibiotics.

Bob didn't go out and get a job. He visited Pamela in the hospital only a couple of times. When he did, he was distant, cold, and buzzed.

Just Left Alone

When Pamela and Bob entered the house, a curtain of silence dropped down between them. Bob went to bed, feeling foolish about running over the souvenirs in the garage. Pamela sat down in the living room, enjoying the silence and solitude. She thought the stress of the evening was over.

Bob came out of the bedroom, sloppily remorseful about making an ass out of himself. He wanted Pamela to come to bed. He wanted to make love to her.

Pamela simply didn't want to. She felt humiliated by his antics. She told him she just wanted to be alone in the living room.

Bob kept pleading for her to come to bed with him. The thought of lying with him repulsed her. She could imagine the alcohol oozing through his pores and making a smelly, sweaty mess on the sheets. Pamela vehemently refused and told Bob to leave her alone.

Bob continued to push the issue. He went to the

refrigerator and cracked open another beer. He entered the dining room and stared vacantly at Pamela in the adjoining living room. He was now pleading with her, telling her how much he loved her and wanted to sleep with her.

Pamela refused for the third time.

Bob became angry and decided to pick a fight.

Warning Signs

In early April 2003, Pamela was still recovering from open-heart surgery. Bob approached her one evening, beer in hand, and told her he wanted to fly his daughter and grandson down to Phoenix from Oregon. Pamela tiredly tried to reason with him by pointing out that they didn't have any money for airline tickets. Pamela couldn't even cover the house payment.

Bob exploded like a Roman candle. His rapid-fire tirade shook her. "You try to ruin everything. You never agree with anything I say. You always try to make me look like the bad guy."

Bob shoved Pamela hard in the shoulder. The staples in her breastbone strained under the force of the thrust. Bob walked off in disgust. When she regained her balance and the pain subsided, she got her purse and the keys to the truck. She had to get away. She thought he needed to cool down. She walked out the door wearing nightclothes and fuzzy slippers.

Pamela got into the pickup truck, drove a couple of blocks, and pulled over. She put her head down on the steering wheel and cried. She thought she needed to find another place to live. She couldn't take this any more.

Bob called her cell phone and told her she needed to find another place to live.

Pamela remembered that she had left her heart medicine at the house. When she returned, she was locked out. She pleaded with Bob through the door until he let her back in.

Pamela lay down on the spare bed. Her chest ached. She cried silently, wondering how her seemingly happy marriage had slowly evaporated. She was done making excuses for Bob. There was no love left in their relationship; they had quit being intimate more than a year before. The situation was getting out of control.

Confrontation in the Kitchen

After Pamela refused to sleep with Bob, he took his nearly full can of beer, sloshed it in her face, and then poured it over her head.

Pamela seethed, "Don't pour your beer on me!"

Bob dropped the half-empty can.

Pamela picked it up and lobbed it at Bob. It bounced off his thigh.

Enraged that she put up a defense, Bob reached down, picked up the can, and hurled it at Pamela. It struck her left hamstring, the very spot where the doctors had harvested the veins for her angioplasty and where infection had set in. Pamela screamed from the throbbing pain and limped into the hallway, trying to get away from Bob.

Bob had thrown the can so hard he fell on an oak icebox and smashed it to pieces. This made him even angrier. He pulled himself back up on his feet.

Pamela turned around in time to see an enraged Bob charging her like a bull, right hand raised and fist clenched. She felt his fist make contact with her lip. Her teeth crunched, and she fell backward.

Becoming a Statistic

According to the Supreme Court of Arizona, one million American women suffer nonfatal violence by an intimate partner each year. While Pamela may not have realized it, she was becoming a statistic. What statistics do not convey is the horror of having a husband turn from being a life partner into an emotional, mental, and physical threat.

AARDVARC (Abuse Rape and Domestic Violence Resource Collection), an online clearinghouse of information about domestic violence, defines four ways Pamela was abused by her husband.

First, Pamela endured emotional and mental abuse when Bob put her down by accusing her of being selfish, calling her ungrateful, and humiliating her in front of mutual friends.

Second, Pamela suffered economic abuse when Bob took her money, called it theirs, and used it for his own purposes.

Third, Bob used privilege when he elevated himself to a position above Pamela by attempting to make all the decisions in the relationship and treating her like a servant.

Finally, Pamela endured physical abuse when Bob pushed her, threw his beer at her, and hit her.

ARRDVARC identifies four traits among men who abuse their partners; all apply to Bob. These men have low self-esteem, are extremely sensitive to mild criticism, blame others for their problems, and use drinking to cope with stress. For Bob, the cycle of unemployment and alcoholism destroyed his self-esteem. Both conditions fed on each other. Because of his low self-esteem, Pamela bore the brunt of the shame and anger generated by Bob's alcoholism and depression. He used his wife as his crutch and enabler, and she ultimately became his victim.

Blood on the Tile

In an instant, Pamela went from watching a fuming, enraged Bob charging her to lying on the dining room floor. Her mouth tasted like salty iron. As her eyes began to focus on the room's white walls, she struggled to her knees. Blood flowed from her mouth. Her lip was split. She could feel with her tongue that teeth were missing.

Pamela managed to stand up and stumble down the hall. Blood stained the taupe tile as she struggled toward the bathroom. She flipped on the cold water in the sink, put her mouth under it, and washed the blood down the drain. Her chest hurt from the impact of hitting the ground. A six-inch bruise was forming where the beer can had hit her leg. Pamela looked in the mirror and cringed at what she saw. Blood oozed from her mouth, which had begun to swell. Her entire body ached – her face, back, and chest – from Bob's slugging her.

Bob, meanwhile, was drunkenly grabbing his clothes in the bedroom. He knew what he had done and was planning a quick exit.

Bob growled at Pamela, half-pleading and half-threatening her. "You better not call the police." He grabbed three armloads of clothes, dumped them into the bed of his pickup truck, and took off.

Pamela cleaned herself up as much as she could. The silence in the house was eerie. Five minutes earlier, it had been a war zone.

Pamela called Tom, Bob's best friend, and he and his girlfriend Jeannie came right over. Jeannie walked into the house and saw the blood trail going down the tile. She looked at Pamela, defeated, scared, and shell-shocked. Jeannie immediately called 911.

Police and Paramedics

Ten minutes later, Officer Angel Gonzalez arrived on the scene to find Pamela, Tom, and Jeannie in the living room. Pamela was nearly catatonic with fright. Officer Gonzalez took down information for his police report. He asked his dispatcher to send a car to look around the neighborhood for Bob's Chevy pickup, but they came up empty.

A first-responder fire truck arrived, and a paramedic treated Pamela. Four upper teeth on the left side of her mouth were missing. Her lip was split halfway to her nose. A purple and yellow bruise was forming over the surgery scars on her leg.

Pamela was in shock and couldn't speak. When Officer Gonzalez asked if she wanted to press charges against Bob, she nodded.

A police photographer took digital photographs of the crime scene – Pamela's split lip and missing teeth, the blood in the hallway and the bathroom. A police officer found Pamela's teeth inside the open closet in the hallway – ten feet away from where she had been hit.

Tom and Jeanie took Pamela to the hospital to get stitched up. Every time she closed her eyes, she cringed, haunted by the image of her enraged husband charging at her with a raised fist.

Reinventing a Ruined Life

Pamela's universe changed drastically after that evening. Bob's violent outburst proved to be the fulcrum of her life – the defining moment. Before Bob hit her, Pamela's life revolved around her marriage. Afterward, her life centered on recovering from Bob. When reflecting back on the process of starting over, Pamela said, "After Bob hit me, I felt like my life was being flushed down the toilet and all of my energy was spent swimming against the current as the bowl drained."

In the year after Bob battered her, Pamela moved seven times. She has struggled with poverty, her health, and her self-esteem. Leaving Bob and her abusive situation was only the beginning of her battle.

Tom and Jeanie took Pamela back to their house at 5:30 a.m. after only a few hours in the hospital. The doctors stitched up her lip, but they couldn't reattach her teeth. The next day, after Tom and Jeanie went to work, she was terrified at being alone in the empty house. Every passing car might be Bob.

Tom was angry with Bob for striking Pamela and wanted to help her get back on her feet. Tom had recently inherited a house from a deceased uncle and offered to let her live there. Instead of paying rent, she would remodel the interior.

Pamela moved in and went to work. She painted most of the interior, wallpapered the kitchen, refurbished the cabinets, and cleaned the carpets – all out of her own pocket. She also packed up the uncle's possessions to pay Tom back for letting her live there rent-free.

About three months after the incident, Tom and Bob began to hang out again. They patched up their differences, and Tom began to sympathize with Bob. When a battered woman like Pamela chooses to leave her abusive situation, her path to emancipation often runs into complications – mutual friends.

Pamela had a hard time paying the utility bills. She made only $1,700 per month as a dispatcher. Between the truck payment, cell phone, health insurance, heart medication, food, and previous medical bills, she had no disposable income. Pamela now felt married to her truck. It was worth less than what she owed on it, but it was her only way to get to work.

Pamela lived in the house for eight months until Tom asked her to move. He gave her a week to find another apartment and move her furniture. He didn't offer to help.

Pamela had to put her household goods into storage and move into Cassie's House, a Christian shelter for abused women in Phoenix. She had to attend church on Sunday and Wednesday. Although not particularly religious, she was grateful to have a place to live.

After a few weeks, Pamela and the other residents were forced to move into a temporary shelter because Cassie's House was approaching its five-year mark of operation and needed to renew its operating license from the state. The temporary shelter, a dilapidated house near the state fairgrounds, was infested with sewer roaches.

Ten days later, Pamela contacted DOVES (Domestic Older Victims Empower and Safety), a Glendale group that helps older victims of domestic violence. Alice Ghareib, the domestic violence program coordinator, helped Pamela find an apartment in an assisted-living home for the physically and mentally disabled and crime victims. The apartment wasn't ready yet, so Pamela had to move into another temporary apartment in the meantime.

Finally, in late April, Pamela moved into her new home.

One year, seven moves.

Bob and the Law

Bob was never punished for what he did to Pamela.

He ran. He grabbed his clothes and ran.

Pamela filed an order of protection on May 12, 2003, the day after Bob struck her. This order prohibited Bob from coming near her, her place of employment, or her home.

Pamela kept pestering the police to investigate her complaint against Bob. Finally, on September 18, 2003, a detective arrested Bob. His brother posted bail. Bob was charged with a felony assault and battery. He pleaded not guilty.

The wheels of justice turned slowly. Finally, on February 5, 2004, the trial started. It lasted six days. Tom spoke for the defense and vouched for Bob. Pamela avoided eye contact with Bob during the trial, which ended in a hung jury. One male juror decided there wasn't enough evidence to prove Bob had hit Pamela, despite the photographs, the testimony of Officer Gonzalez, and Pamela's own testimony.

The judge was furious at the outcome.

In the case of a hung jury, another jury must be selected and the case must be tried over again. While the case was in the process of going to trial again, Bob accepted a plea bargain and pled guilty to one misdemeanor count of assault and battery. He is still awaiting sentencing.

Pamela wants a clean break from Bob financially, legally, and emotionally, but her financial circumstances make a proper divorce impossible. She can't afford a divorce attorney to file for a contested divorce, yet she makes just enough money to disqualify her from free legal assistance from the state.

She has received paralegal assistance from the state of Arizona, but the counselor could only give her guidance, not advice. To be free from Bob's financial debt, Pamela must find a pro bono divorce attorney to take on her case. She's still looking.

In the meantime, Bob lives in their house with his girlfriend.

The Road Ahead

Pamela can't fathom how her life spiraled into her current situation. She is deeply embarrassed about her missing teeth and scarred lip. She is humiliated every time she has to tell her story at one government agency or another, trying to get legal help or basic necessities. She feels like a refugee every time she returns to her assisted-living apartment. She lost her family and her identity. Pamela is a defeated victim from an unjust and undeclared war.

Pamela gets up in the morning and goes to work out of habit. Something inside her keeps her functioning. It's an innate, almost unconscious hope that things will someday get better. She wants a normal, fulfilling life once again. As her tongue feels the empty space where four teeth should be, she wonders, "I'm a good person, aren't I? It has to get better."

roadside respects

Drew Bratcher, University of Missouri

The second week of March has not been good for John Stone – another sub-par week following a sub-par month in which he only picked up 16 deer, nine fewer than his average. Most people don't measure their months in deer, but for Stone each road-killed deer is $40, and nine below average is a $360 hit.

At 42 years old, with short hair, short sideburns and a thin beard and mustache the color of a freshly paved road, Stone is a deer cleanup specialist who couldn't care less about the squirrels, rabbits, skunks, dogs, possums, raccoons, snakes, armadillos, blown-out tires or any other inanimate object that has been known to occupy a Missouri road shoulder. Stone is a deer man in a city where it pays to be one. According to the Department of Conservation, in 2003 Boone County roads were the reported death sites of at least 463 deer, many of which took their last breath on Columbia roads.

Stone won his year-long contract, the only one issued by the Department of Conservation for deer cleanup in Columbia, last summer because he offered the lowest bid – $35 less than the next lowest bidder. But he made up the difference during the next year when on some days he'd load the rack on the back of his gold Chevy truck with up to eight deer carcasses.

However, by the end of the second week of March, Stone begins to accept that maybe the drastic changes in the weather – warm and sunny one hour and chilly and cloudy the next – had kept young bucks from trying their hooves at outrunning headlights. But at 4:30 p.m. Thursday he gets a call. A deer is down off Chapel Hill Road. It isn't much, but it is $40 toward making the week bearable, a modest prize at the end of winter.

When he cruises by on Friday morning, he sees it. Because the deer is small, he decides to pick it up on his way home from the construction site where he's been working as part of a three-man crew remodeling a dilapidated Columbia home. Once the conservation department, which must first receive a call from the public, calls Stone, he has 24 hours to scoop up the deer. If he can find it. Some scavengers, animal and otherwise, have been known to beat Stone to the scene, robbing him of his collection and leaving a bloodstain in its place.

On Friday afternoon, when he and the crew get to a stopping point, Stone throws his tools in the metal box in his truck bed, mounts the truck and steers it into the bumper-car track of rush hour in Columbia. The dust that hovers over tire-whipped gravel roads on early spring days covers Stone's truck like sugar on a donut. The dirty Chevy is more than an extended cab, bed, tires and rack. Stone's truck is his moving connection between carpentry and deer cleanup.

Inside, dirt-matted seats lie beneath root beer-colored windows littered with deer stickers. Above the window of the same door panel that's chalked with sawdust and bleached from sunshine, Stone keeps pictures of his two boys and the deer they killed. The one thing Stone loves more than shooting deer himself is watching his boys shoot them. Fingerprints mark the bent left corner of the picture of his youngest son holding up an eight-pointer. On lunch breaks and while waiting at stop lights, Stone has pulled the picture down and shown it to many passengers.

Stone wears his jacket — the type worn by little league

baseball coaches and copied by renegade kids who spend $1.50 at thrift stores to look retro — for the same reason he wears his ink-blue jeans and striped Adidas shoes: it's functional. He speaks with the sincere and occasional slang and swear of the Midwest that comes out clean no matter how dirty it gets. Most Columbians don't know Stone, but they'd know if he didn't do his job. If he worked in a slaughterhouse, he'd be the guy who keeps the floors clear. As it is, he helps keep Columbia from looking like a slaughterhouse.

But the real work is disposing of the deer once he's racked them up. Stone decides among five options: Dig a hole and bury them; cover them with brush and burn them; put them out as bait for coyote hunting; take them to D-D Farm and feed them to the big cats; or, if the deer are too rotted to be moved in one piece, drag them into a nearby ditch and pour lime on them. Stone often waits until the morning after he picks them up to dispose of carcasses. In the meantime, the deer go anywhere Stone goes: the bank, the grocery store, the gas station.

One day he stopped at Dairy Queen before disposing of a carcass. The deer's legs and head were dangling off the rack and polluting the thought of ice cream for anyone in the parking lot who happened to catch a whiff of the dead animal rising up on the afternoon air. Within moments, a conservation department officer pulled up, handcuffs jingling against the driver-side window.

"What's the deal with this deer on the back of your truck?" the officer asked, ready to take the necessary action. Possession of a road-killed deer requires a disposition form that can be obtained by the Department of Conservation. "I'm the guy who picks them up," Stone said. The officer's eyes dipped down behind his sunglasses and came back,

"Oh, OK. You're John."

"Yessir," Stone said. The officer swore it was the first time he'd met Stone and told him he appreciated his work. Looking him straight in the eyes, he firmly shook Stone's hand, the same hand that gripped a deer carcass minutes earlier.

Most days are not as eventful. On this Friday, he pulls his truck over, cautiously opens the squeaking door to avoid becoming roadkill himself and slaps a yellow strobe light on the roof.

"Yep. It's a button buck, 1-year-old. Would have sprouted antlers next year if he'd made it," says Stone, touching the stubs buried beneath the fur between its ears. If the deer had been older and sprouted antlers that hadn't been thieved before he got there, Stone would have skull-capped it and added the horns to his massive collection. Antlers once graced the walls of his den, when he had one. Now they rest in a box and are spilling onto the floor in the corner of his parent's garage because a recent divorce robbed him of his trophy room. In the box, there is a seven-point rack that Stone cut from a road-killed deer, only three points less than the largest rack that once looked out over his den. Some people would have sold the antlers or ground them into a tincture that happens to be a popular natural aphrodisiac, but for Stone the antlers are simply a nice trophy, a small perk that sometimes comes with the job.

A black stream of blood runs from the yearling's left ear into the dark puddle near its eye. The deer has been dead for several days, and the stench is enough to make the tough-stomached Stone, a man known to plunge his hands into a deer's gut to warm them on cold hunting mornings, cringe.

A memory flashes in his mind. Last summer he'd gone to pick up a doe, and an army of plundering maggots, sensing new flesh, soon turned on him quicker than static hopping across a television screen when the cable cuts out. He almost lost his stomach when the adrenaline he'd exerted from swatting the parasites away wore off.

"Just go ahead and multiply the smell of this one here by three in the summer," he says, pulling his rubber gloves over his hands. A passing truck with a loud muffler lets out a honk. Stone throws up a wave, unsure if the driver knows him or was simply thanking him for his service. For the first time all week, he is happy it is March. Sure it had been a disappointing month, full of deer dashing to safety across car-sparse streets, but at least he doesn't have to resort to the stick-and-a-spoon method, which is the term used to explain the process of shoveling up a sun-melted deer in the summer months, meaning you need a stick and a spoon to do the job. Picking them up is like trying to eat soup with a fork.

He rolls the lifeless beauty over to get a good enough handle to toss it onto the rack like a bag of dog food, and blood erupts like lava out of the buck's ear and onto Stone's shoes. He doesn't flinch. He holds the deer in his arms in a paternal way, aimed at securing some sort of dignity for the animal despite the idiocy and sloppiness of its death. As a man in touch with nature, Stone is a throwback colliding with contemporary Columbia. And in that sense, he's not so unlike the deer he scoops up. He's a deer lover, and deer lovers love deer to the bloodiest end.

It's not until the dead animal is on the rack, where nearly 200 deer have lain before, that Stone finally notices his shoes. He wipes his mustache with the back of his hand, and is assured that in the same way that the jet-propelled wind would shortly blow away the blood-smeared leaves the deer has left behind, the fresh blood on his shoes is nothing a little bleach can't make white again.

a habit that sucks?

Paige Greenfield, Northwestern University

Katie Lowes, a 22-year-old actress, travels across Manhattan from auditions to rehearsals to performances to meetings with agents. Each time she boards the subway, she shuffles into a vacant seat, and as her wavy chestnut hair tumbles in front of her face, she sneaks her left thumb into her mouth until she reaches her next stop. "It's an extremely calming habit," says Lowes, who has sucked since ultrasounds depicted her thumb-in-mouth in utero. "Although it could lead to crooked teeth, it doesn't kill you like smoking cigarettes, or heroin or crack."

Lowes sucks her thumb throughout the day, but mostly at night when she returns home exhausted. She types on the computer using one hand while sucking her other thumb. Before going on stage, Lowes indulges to calm her nerves. Her mother jokes that, when she becomes famous, Jay Leno will taunt her with photographic evidence of her sucking habit. "I wouldn't care," says Lowes. "It's who I am, it's what I do."

Few adults will admit to clinging to their childish habits. But when they fall asleep clutching their tattered teddy or wash-cloth sized security blanket, or sneak into the bathroom during work for a quick thumb-suck, the truth emerges: some have never abandoned their childhood habits. In fact, more than 250,000 U.S. adults suck their thumbs, says Harvey Miller, 53, who runs thumbsucking-adults.com. In a typical week, Miller's website averages 1,200 hits. While all visitors may not be thumb-suckers, the website alone can change people's views about the social stigma attached to adult thumb-sucking.

The habit is becoming increasingly visible in public

spaces, in literature, in movies and especially on the Internet. With the summer 2005 release of the film Thumbsucker, featuring Keanu Reeves, Benjamin Bratt and Vince Vaughn, it will receive national exposure. Thumbsucker, based on the 1999 comedic novel of the same title by former New York Magazine book critic Walter Kirn, is a coming-of-age tale about a teen thumb-sucker who turns to his hippie orthodontist (Reeves) and high school debate coach to conquer his habit.

Miller, a business owner in East Meadow, N.Y., who sucks his thumb, launched thumbsuckingadults.com in Sept. 1998. His inspiration came during a two-week Florida vacation, where he witnessed three different women thumb-sucking in public. He searched the Internet and discovered a site exploring this phenomenon, but the webmaster was shutting it down because his girlfriend was unhappy with his frequent communication with other women. Miller created a new site, and six years later thumbsuckingadults.com is the only resource of its kind.

The website features an extensive Frequently Asked Questions section, ranging from thumb-suckers' inquiries about disclosing their habit to their partners to why they have continued sucking and whether they should quit. There are links devoted to celebrities who publicly admit to sucking their thumbs, including Kyra Sedgwick, Suzanne Sommers and Rosanna Arquette, and even those who have been photographed seductively with thumb-in-mouth, such as Madonna and Courtney Love. Most significantly, thumbsuckingadults.com has evolved into a support group for those who indulge. The members post messages on the website's forum and connect with each other.

Miller jokingly highlights the habit's advantages, pointing out that it is legal, moral and calorie and carbohydrate-free. Thumb-sucking can enable a person to think better, to sleep under a variety of conditions and possesses no ill health effects, he says. Psychologist Dr. Susan Heitler, although critical of the habit, adds that thumb-sucking "can be tempting because it is genuinely physiologically soothing and is probably less detrimental than smoking for being a soothing habit." It affects brain waves, lowers the heart-rate, and releases the same brain chemicals as meditation, says Heitler.

Thumb-suckers across America agree: this is their relaxation method. Lowes, who will star in a July episode of a new FX dramatic-comedy, Rescue Me, and will play Juliet in the New Canaan Shakespeare Festival's production of Romeo and Juliet in Connecticut this summer, says that she always has the ability to calm herself in the palm of her hand. Deon Rodden, a 22-year-old thumb-sucker and computer consultant from Boca Raton, Fla., echoes Lowes' sentiment. "It has a calming effect," he says. "My heart beat slows down, it makes me more relaxed, helps me when I'm extra stressed and makes me fall asleep."

Fifteen years ago, Eric, 47, who requested that his last name be omitted because he worries he will be judged for his habit, rediscovered thumb-sucking after more than a decade-long hiatus. Out of curiosity, he placed his left thumb into his mouth. "It was like a bolt of lightening," he says. "I thought, 'I forgot how nice this can be.'" Eric, an entertainment executive in Los Angeles, Calif., sucks his thumb throughout the day. "It's not like I walk down the street with my thumb in my mouth," he says. But when stressed, he closes his office door or huddles in a bathroom stall to privately indulge.

But the question remains: What makes these adult thumb-suckers different from those who stopped before their age reached a whole hand? Heitler, author of David Decides: No More Thumbsucking, says that most children should and do stop before they are 3 or 4 years old. "Most people are tuned in to what's appropriate," she says. Thumb-sucking as an adult is "age inappropriate" and is probably the result of "excessively permissive parents, which encourages children to stay on and on." Lowes' parents never approved of her thumb-sucking, but, she says, "I think they've given up."

Miller attributes adult thumb-sucking to a cost/benefit ratio in which the calming effects outweigh any negatives, such as dental problems, calluses and embarrassment. Thumb-suckers capable of hiding their habit enjoy the benefits without negative reactions from others. "Still some, the confident ones, have the attitude that they have a right to thumb-suck, especially since they weren't hurting anyone," says Miller. And some continue because their habit is part of their identity. "It's really my thing," says Lowes. "I'm an actress. I'm a thumb-sucker."

Heitler likens thumb-sucking to the rhythmic activity of sitting in a rocking chair. Both actions are mindless and soothing. Susan O'Neill, 27, a first grade teacher at a Chicago elementary school, says the habit comforts her, especially when she's tired or upset. "That's why I never stopped," she says. "It makes me relax, it calms me down." Rodden, who often works during the night and sleeps at erratic hours, says thumb-sucking gives him the flexibility to nod off at different times. "I find it very difficult to sleep without it; it's my procedure," he says.

But thumb-sucking has its disadvantages. Rodden wore braces when he was 17 to correct the overbite that thumb-sucking caused. But he admits that his dental problems, which cost more than $5,000, did not incite a desire to quit. "Braces are worth the cost," he says. When Lowes was 11 years old, thumb-sucking resulted in an infected gland on the inside of her lower lip from her thumb rubbing against her bottom teeth. The gland swelled to a bubble that had to be removed through surgery. She has also worn a retainer and currently wears Invisalign braces, removable clear molds placed over her teeth to correct their crookedness. Lowes' sucking-related dental problems ring up to at least $7,000.

Many adult thumb-suckers attempted to quit when they were younger but determined that trying to quit was not worth the struggle. Lowes tried breaking her habit through numerous methods but each failed. At 10, she tried covering her thumbs with Band-Aids, but instead she sucked right through them. At night she rubbed a bitter-tasting substance, Thumb/Off, onto her thumbs, but discovered that sucking her thumb for five minutes would eliminate the awful taste and then "it would be smooth sailing," says Lowes. Some thumb-suckers go to more extreme lengths to quit. A retainer-like dental appliance called a "fence" can be bonded to the palate, removing the pleasurable, sucking action that thumb-suckers enjoy.

Despite past efforts, most thumb-suckers do not want to stop. Miller says many people visit the website with intentions to quit, but once they look at the material and realize they are not alone, they almost invariably decide to continue. "The only reason they quit is because of outside values placed on them," says Miller.

For many adult thumb-suckers, the social stigma attached to thumb-sucking frustrates them. Eric, who has been married for 20 years, says he wishes thumb-sucking was socially acceptable. "People are so individual," he says. "They have other habits – cigarette smoking, nail-biting

– different characteristics of our personalities that make us predisposed to certain habits." Thumb-suckers, he says, are just like everyone else. Rodden, whose thumb's calming effects help him to relax and fall asleep, sees no end to the habit. "If anyone felt what I feel when I suck my thumb they'd never want to stop," he says.

Thumb-suckers disagree about whether their habit is indicative of a bold or weak character. While Miller contends that public thumb-sucking is a sign of confidence, Natasha Johns, 26, a human resource specialist for the federal government, insists that she is "a weaker person." Some people can stop cold turkey, says Johns, but "I'm just one of those people who's a little weaker, and continues to hold on to thumb-sucking." But Anji Petroski, 35, a stay-at-home mom, sees it differently. "I don't have a baby complex," she says. "I'm a very aggressive female. It's something that I couldn't break and didn't want to break. We're not hurting anybody by doing it, we don't infringe on anyone, it's not a big deal."

For many thumb-suckers, using accessory objects is another component of their habit. Some suck with a beloved security blanket while others rub silk fabrics, like women's nightgowns or bra straps. For ultimate comfort, Rodden sucks his thumb while lounging upon over-stuffed feather down pillows. Fifteen years ago, when taking a cloth diaper out of the dryer, Eric, a father of now an 11 and 18-year-old, noticed that it was too thin and holey to be used anymore. He stuck his left ring finger through one of the holes, lifted his thumb to his mouth and started sucking. "It was a piece of the missing puzzle," says Eric. He cut off a section and used it for about five years until it shredded. Within another five years, Eric went through another piece and figures he has a few months left with the current segment. The more worn the cloth becomes, the more Eric says he loves its softness and the odor that he can only describe as "being very uniquely it." To prolong the cloth's life, he washes it in a net bag designed for delicates, and dreads the prospect of starting a new piece. The three-inch cloth is tattered, frayed and dotted with holes. Eric says that it is the perfect size to bunch into his hand and keeps it in his left pants pocket during the day. The accessory, he explains, is a companion to his habit: "My thumb-sucking doesn't feel as complete without it and it doesn't feel as complete without my thumb-sucking."

To the chagrin of many thumb-suckers, celebrities, such as Madonna and Courtney Love, have used the habit to sell albums. According to a section of Miller's website, "Why it's Sexy," thumb-sucking's sexualization is to be expected since it focuses on the "sensual oral center…and so much of what is human has become sexualized in one way or another." A 56-year-old man, who spoke on the condition of anonymity, says he finds thumb-sucking women "very erotic." When he was in graduate school, he accidentally caught his girlfriend, a CEO of a large company, thumb-sucking during the night. "I have since come to the conclusion that my erotic experience may have been that by her sucking her thumb – so totally out of character from her powerful woman, independent image – she showed a human and a bit vulnerable side that I enjoyed," he says. "But wow, it was an intense feeling."

Thumb-suckers can face a difficult challenge when revealing their habit to their partners. Johns has had the same boyfriend for three years, but never told him that she sucks her thumb. She makes sure that she is alone or waits for him to fall asleep at night before sneaking her left thumb into her mouth. In the past, boyfriends left because of her habit, so she decided to avoid the risk with this relationship. "At first they think it's cute," says Johns. "But once they realize how involved it is they've broken up with me." For Lowes, sucking her thumb in front of others depends on her comfort level. "If I'm comfortable around you, then I'll suck my thumb around you," she says. Lowes has had steady boyfriends since age 15, and has been dating the same man for more than four years. "No one has ever had a problem with it. They find it kind of cute, become used to it and stop noticing," she says. Rodden's fiancée is not as comfortable with his habit. "At first she was OK with it," he says. "Now she seems to be somewhat jealous. I'll be lying next to her sucking my thumb, and she feels she has to compete with it."

When Miller began the website, he corresponded with a 44-year-old woman who never admitted her habit to her spouse. She said that she would rather her husband find out she was having an affair than know that she sucked her thumb. Heitler warns that thumb-sucking can be detrimental to a person's mental health if it is kept a secret. "Those adults who would be embarrassed if the habit was public can hold them back from relationships if a woman doesn't want a man to know she sucks her thumb at night," says Heitler. She adds that thumb-suckers have failed to develop effective ways of dealing with everyday stresses and resort to their habit for relaxation. "Being able to think in a constructive way about what the stresses are, living life in a pace that's calming enough or putting on upbeat or soothing music are more age-appropriate calming methods for adults," says Heitler.

Still, many adult thumb-suckers across America intend to continue their habit and are increasingly taking it out from under the covers. Thumbsuckingadult.com's forum is as active as ever with 835 members posting more than 30 messages each week. Miller is currently processing 2,500 surveys he administered to thumb-suckers over the past five years. The responses, he hopes, will shed light on the characteristics of those who share the habit.

In a country where 23 percent of the adult population smokes despite its deadly consequences, it is curious that smoking continues to be socially acceptable. Perhaps we would all be healthier if we exchanged our Marlboros, Big Macs and Miller for our thumbs.

surviving the guilt

James Carlson, University of Missouri

John Krogh woke from the flashback with a shudder. God, won't these ever stop? His short, cropped white hair glistened with sweat, and his blue eyes peered around the hospital room.

Please God, give me the strength to endure.

That uneasy feeling swept over him again. Guilt. A heavy blanket of guilt weighing him down. Guilt because he is 69 and alive. Guilt because they were younger and are now dead. He wished for the times back home when he'd go to bed dreaming of his next home-improvement project.

His home in Utah sits on a plateau atop a canyon on the outskirts of Wallsburg, which is 56 miles away from Salt Lake City. Outside his back-facing window pine trees dot the snow-capped mountains of the Wasatch Range. Through the windows in his bedroom, the sagebrush valley rolls down to Wallsburg three miles away. Deer and elk trod through the area often.

The house John and his wife, Karen, built was complete in anyone else's eyes. But as John lay down every night for bed, visions of the next task bounced around his head: crown moldings and baseboards, cabinets and maybe a fireplace in the basement. He used to picture it all.

Not anymore.

Lying in a Missouri hospital 1,200 miles from his canyon-side home, he could only picture the horror. Every time he closed his eyes, it was there. The dead woman across his lap. The burning plane. The guilt.

What if ... what if ... what if ...

On Tuesday, Oct. 19, 2004 commuter airplane Flight 5966 crashed into a wooded area near the Kirksville airport. The largest section of the plane that remained intact was burned to only ashes as firefighters fought the flames throughout the evening. Of the 15 on board, only two survived. (Courtesy of Al Maglio/Kirksville Daily Express)

Just a Medical Conference

John gathered his luggage on October 19, 2004 and headed for his front door. He grabbed his wallet, keys and Listerine Cool Mint PocketPaks from a table by the entrance. He was flying to Missouri.

He had no idea he'd soon be on the country's deadliest flight in 2004 — the deadliest flight in Missouri since 1973. He didn't know his plane would be one of four to go down in Missouri in October, a period that left 20 dead and only three survivors. And he didn't know that he, the oldest on any of the flights, would be one of those three. He was just flying to a medical conference.

John had taught at the Kirksville College of Osteopathic Medicine for 23 years, and while there, he won multiple teaching awards for his excellent relationships with students. Clark Ator was one of those students.

Clark attended the same Church of Jesus Christ of Latter-Day Saints in Kirksville as John and his wife, and the two began playing basketball and attending church events together. But it was Clark's generous personality that really drew John to him. Two years later Clark became a doctor, and when one of John's students couldn't find a physician to do rounds with, Clark would always offer his services. Clark later joined the staff of the Kirksville College of Osteopathic Medicine and became a regional assistant dean in Utah with John.

The first leg of John's flight took him into St. Louis. Seven other employees from the college's regional offices around the country gathered to board the plane to Kirksville. John said hello to Mark Varidin, another of John's former students who was now the regional assistant dean in Florida.

John walked up the tarmac's portable staircase and into Corporate Airlines' 19-seat turboprop jet, Flight 5966. There was a one-seat row to the left of the aisle and a two-seat row on the right. John chose the emergency row on the right. Here he could stretch out his 6-foot-1-inch frame in the extra space.

As he sat down by the window, Wendy Bonham, his assistant from Utah, leaned over from her seat left of the aisle.

"We've got assigned seats, and I'm not sure that's yours," she said. John peered around the plane.

"I'm the last one on, so I don't think it will matter," John replied.

They were in the air at 6:45 p.m.

Flight 5966 had 10 people traveling to the seminar in Kirksville, eight of them from the college's regional offices. Two photographers and a history teacher were also on board. The 13 passengers came from Texas and Utah, Michigan and Ohio, New York and Florida. One of those 13, sitting less than 10 feet from John, was 39-year-old Clark Ator.

Up front, the two pilots were beginning their 14th hour on duty and sixth flight of the day.

This can't be happening

Three women carried on a lively conversation near the front of the plane, but the roaring engine prevented John from hearing much. He turned his attention out the window.

Patches of fog passed by in the darkening night, and

John thought of a time 17 years earlier when Karen had been flying into Kirksville. The cloud cover was too heavy then, and the pilot had to turn around.

John heard the landing gear extend and snapped out of his thoughts. His daughter, Janelle, and grandchildren were waiting at the airport. John tried to reach in his pants pocket for his Listerine strips. He couldn't reach them with his seat belt on and decided to wait until they landed.

He crossed his legs and leaned over to tell Wendy about Karen's foggy flight.

BANG!

Before he could open his mouth, there was a loud metallic crash like a car tearing into a tin shed. People screamed. This couldn't be happening, could it? People were talking a moment ago. No sudden loss of altitude. Just a crash. Seconds later, a series of staccato bumps. No one screamed now; they didn't have the breath.

The plane rattled. The lights flickered. John gripped his armrests. More jolting knocks. More loud thumps. Then nothing. The pilots had radioed Kansas City's regional control tower at 7:27 p.m. to say the flight was going fine. According to the National Transportation Safety Board, the plane crashed 10 minutes later in a wooded patch four miles from the airport. Visibility on the ground was excellent, but a thick cloud cover hovered 300 feet above the airport. It's possible the pilots didn't see the trees until it was too late.

The Terrain Awareness and Warning System, a device that alerts pilots to obstacles in their path, such as trees, will be required on all commercial planes with six seats or more by March 29. Before the crash, Corporate Airlines had installed the system on two of its 11 planes. John's flight was not one of them.

John woke up to a smoky cabin. Papers, luggage and clothes were strewn everywhere. A single person groaned. John took a breath. The haze singed his nostrils and burned his eyes. There was a weight on his lap, and he looked down. A woman in a red sweater and a brown leather jacket lay across his knees. Blood covered her arm and hand, and she wasn't moving.

Was he the only survivor? That couldn't be.

He looked to his left and saw light pouring in from an opening. He had to get out. He moved the woman and fell to the ground. His hip was broken. He struggled across the aisle.

Wendy's voice rang out.

"Dr. Krogh! Dr. Krogh!"

She was alive! If he could stand on the wing outside, maybe he could pull some people out. There was hope. But when he stuck his head out the opening, his heart sank. The wing was gone, and the plane was lodged 8 feet off the ground in a patch of oak and hickory trees. His hip screamed at him, and he made the only decision he could. He threw himself out.

Falling eight feet, he landed on his head. Perhaps this is when he broke his back and ribs. Flames from burning debris tickled his feet, and he immediately crawled away on his back. The 69-year-old man with a broken hip, a broken back and broken ribs mustered all his upper body strength to distance himself from the fire. He saw another figure appear at the opening and tumble out. He'd later learn it was Wendy, who would also survive. He struggled on 25 feet through a rose thicket that tore at his skin until he couldn't continue.

John looked up through the thorny bush at the fuselage stuck in the tree.

BOOM!

The plane spit plumes of fire toward the heavens. The canary-yellow leaves of autumn scattered about the ground became, for a moment, illuminated by the burst of flames. Molten plastic rained down, burning his legs and feet.

Minutes passed, and the explosions slowed. The night crackled with small fires. Less than a foot from John's face, a mouse scurried across the thorny branches. This whole thing didn't make sense. He had lived 69 good years. So many people on the plane had lived only half that.

The situation slowly took hold of John. Tears trickled down his cheeks. Mark Varidin left behind a wife and child. Clark left behind a wife and seven children. John lost it.

He sobbed and sobbed. For the people he knew: Mark and Clark. For the people he didn't: Richard Sarkin, Steven Miller, Judith Diffenderfer, M. Bridget Wagner, Toni Sarantino, Kathleen Gebard, Matthew Johnson, Paul Talley, Rada Bronson, Kim Sasse and Jonathan Palmer. He cried for their families left behind. He cried for the years they would not live. Lying in pain in a patch of thorns in the middle of a northern Missouri field, John cried for everything.

More than 20 minutes passed before John heard rustling.

"Confirmed sighting of downed aircraft," someone said.

"Over here, over here," John managed to squeak. His voice came out no louder than telephone-conversation level. Finally, someone stumbled across his bloody body, and rescuers gathered around him.

Troy Mihalevich, a flight paramedic, leaned over John.

"I used to wrestle with your son, Dr. Krogh," he said.

John was safe now, but his emotional journey had just begun.

Part of the pilots' log book, recovered only 15 feet

from the burning wreckage, remained intact after a large portion of the plane's body was destroyed. Pieces of the manifest scattered for 5 or 10 feet around the area, and the pages that weren't incinerated are being used as evidence in the pending lawsuits. (Courtesy of Al Maglio/Kirksville Daily Express)

A Guilty Conscience

In a dark room filled with beeping machines at Northeast Regional Medical Center in Kirksville, John tried to sleep. His conscience, however, would not allow him to. When his eyes shut, his mind opened to the crash.

Debris floating around the foggy cabin. Light pouring in from the left. The bloodied woman across his knees and the balls of fire shooting into the sky.

He could picture it all. His faith told him to pray.

Please God, give me the strength to endure.

During the day, John's psychiatrist Dr. Andrew Lovy just listened. John talked through what had happened, and the doctor nodded. It was good to talk, the doctor said.

But couldn't John think about something else for just a minute? What about the cabinets and crown moldings and fireplaces that awaited him back in Utah? He longed to think of that again, to dream of the next project. But his mind wouldn't allow him such a reprieve.

Two weeks after the crash, Travis Lee, a respiratory therapist, visited John's room for a checkup. When Travis mentioned the crash, John sniffled then choked up. He reached up with his hand, latched onto Travis' neck and pulled him into an embrace. John sobbed and stammered, "If only I hadn't broken my hip, I could have helped them."

John's fingers dug into the therapist's neck. His voice caught as he tried to get his breath. He sobbed on Travis's shoulder. If John could hold onto him long enough, maybe things would be different.

"If only I hadn't broken my hip, I could have helped them," he repeated. "If only I hadn't broken my hip."

John didn't want to let go. He couldn't let go.

Please God, give me the strength to endure. Give me the strength to endure.

A couple of days later he sat down with Dr. Lovy. Up to this point, John had done most of the talking. It was good to get it out, right? But John had gotten it out. He had talked about it, and still the blanket of guilt choked him.

He hadn't sat in his assigned seat. He had kept his seat belt on instead of taking it off. He had crossed his legs seconds before the crash. One doctor said this caused his left leg, not his head, to take the brunt of the impact. Plus he was the oldest person on the plane by 15 years.

There were so many reasons to say "if only," so many reasons to ask why. Why did he survive? Why did Clark, 30 years younger, die? If only he hadn't broken his hip, maybe he could have ...

But when this session started, Dr. Lovy didn't just listen.

"How long did it take you to get out of there?" the doctor asked.

"Just seconds," John said.

"How bad was the smoke?"

"It was bad. It burned my eyes, burned my nose."

"If you were able to bring the people to the opening, what would you have done?"

"I guess I would have thrown them out."

"Do you think they were already dead? Would they have survived the fall? How would you have dragged them away from the flames?"

John didn't say anything else. He let the doctor's words roll around in his head. On November 12, three weeks after the crash, John, with a walker rolling in front of him, limped out to a motor home where his two sons, Benjamin and Frank, were standing.

The two packed the walker into the motor home's closet, helped John into the vehicle and began the journey 1,200 miles back to his home in Utah. The doctor's words continued to replay in John's mind.

The Road to Recovery

It was December, two months removed from the crash. John sat up from the sofa, walked to the TV and turned off the 10 o'clock news. His left leg hitching with each step, he walked toward the staircase of his Utah home.

He passed the windows that looked out on the snow-capped mountains. He limped up the stairs and into his bedroom where the windows looked out over the valley. He crawled into bed and pulled the covers up around his neck.

John had talked with Clark's wife, Karlene, the day after Thanksgiving. The autopsy showed no smoke in Clark's lungs. He died on impact.

The weight was lifting from John's shoulders. With his wife beside him, John turned out the lights, closed his eyes and pictured it all again.

Knotty wood around a fireplace in the basement. That's what the house needed next.

all hail the queens

Misty Huber, University of Kansas

Alexus calls me to say she's stuck in traffic on her way to Lawrence from Kansas City, Mo., and she'll be a few minutes late to our 6:30 p.m. interview. This is my first time talking to Alexus Panache. She directs the "Alexus Panache Show," a once-a-month drag show at Jack Flanigan's Bar & Grill, 806 W 24th St., hosted on Wednesday's alternative lifestyles night. Before today I had only talked to her male alter ego, Dan Fulk, a freelance makeup artist for Estée Lauder and M.A.C cosmetics.

I arrive at Jack Flanigan's Bar & Grill at 6:35 p.m., surprised to see that Alexus is already there. "A queen is never late," she tells me. "Everyone else is just early." She is wearing a green sleeveless t-shirt, baggy shorts and flip-flops, with a flawless French-tipped pedicure. She has comedy and tragedy masks tattooed on her upper arm. She and another performer, Montana, are eating Sonic. They're already in heavy makeup and false eyelashes, preparing for tonight's show, but they tell me they aren't even close to ready. We sit down at a table as the two dig into their fast-food bags.

Alexus tells me she got into drag on a dare from a group of friends. She did theater in high school, and became interested in makeup, entertaining and dancing. "Drag is just another form of theater," she explains. I notice she keeps referring to me as "honey" or "sweetie." She went through many looks before creating Alexus Panache. She picked the name from the "Dynasty" character Alexis Carrington, played by Joan Collins, and panache, which is a French word for "pizzazz." She did her first show in April 2001. Now she does the drag shows at Flanigan's, and occasionally at Tootsies, 1822 Main St., Kansas City, Mo. Still, she says, drag is more a paid hobby than a lifestyle. Alexus is only a small part of Dan, she says. As Alexus, she says she's a little cattier and more fabulous. She likes glitter, glamour and looking pretty.

Alexus tells me a stereotype she faces is that people think she wants to be a woman. She also says she doesn't do drag for a sexual kick, and she doesn't do sexual things with men as Alexus. Montana tells me there's even a stigma in the gay community that all queens are whores. This perception of immorality seems strange when I find out Montana does drag on Sunday nights and gives all the profits to the Kansas City Free Health Clinic, 5119 E. 24th St., Mo.

Montana chose her drag name from a character in the 1991 movie Soapdish. She's been doing drag for 16 years. At age 21 Derek Dyer, Montana's male name, was working at a gay bar in Kansas City, Mo., where he met drag show director, Miss Sandy Kaye. "She did a Judy Garland you would not believe," Montana says. Derek was fascinated that men could look like women. He moved to San Francisco, where he made a living just doing drag, but missed his family in the Kansas City area. He moved back and is again working with his "drag mother," Miss Kaye, and managing an apartment complex. Montana does drag two to three times a week in Kansas City, Mo. She says there is no difference between her and Derek. "I'm the same person on the inside," she says. "There's no emotional change."

Beauty is Pain
The girls have converted the women's bathroom into their dressing room. The smell of hairspray is thick as Montana fluffs a wig on a plastic foam head. Alexus keeps her stage makeup in a huge electrical box; inside are M.A.C

cosmetics and Ben Nye stage makeup. "Cover Girl is to cover a girl, not a boy, honey," she says. They keep their costumes in large blue plastic storage bins. Because the clothes they need are made to fit women's bodies, they have to make a few modifications, such as buying strapless tops to accommodate their wider shoulders, or making their own drag clothes, as Alexus does.

The drag transformation is painful, but you get used to it, Alexus says. Demonstrating how she creates cleavage, she grips the sides of her chest with one hand, and pinches them together. She tapes her faux cleavage with clear packing tape before she stuffs. Drag queens also have to tuck their male genitalia between their legs, and if they're wearing something skimpy, they use duct tape to hold it in place. I wince, but Alexus just shrugs. To avoid shaving their legs, some queens wear up to 10 pairs of pantyhose, Alexus says, but she can get away with a pair of dance tights covered with a pair of nude fishnets. She also glues her heavy jewelry to her skin to keep it from falling off during her dance routines.

Three GQ-esque young men show up to help Alexus and Montana set up their stage. Brandon Prusa, Ulyssus sophomore, says he's helped with all of the shows since he met Alexus last year at Flanigans. He's gay, but not an aspiring queen, he says. Alexus and Montana hang black and red curtains to create a backstage area, while singing to No Doubt's "Just a Girl." Still in their male clothes, they are stapling brightly colored fabric to the curtains. Alexus jokes, "Don't make me get butch." In not much longer than an hour, they have set up a stage and catwalk on the dance floor, complete with a pole.

At about 10 p.m., two more performers arrive, almost in full costume. Desiree Luv is a voluptuous 24-year veteran who does a lot of character drag, invoking Tina Turner and Patti LaBelle. She tells me there's an art to female impersonation; one that's transformed into a beauty competition. She is the only transsexual of the group. She says she has always felt very feminine and as a child everyone always thought she was female. The difference between her and the other girls is the lifestyle, she says. Desiree lives as a woman, she has size 38 C breasts from hormone therapy, but hasn't had sexual-reassignment surgery. She performs in drag shows six nights a week and runs a party bus, called the Mudslide, in Kansas City, Mo. Her transformation to drag takes less time, just 20 minutes.

The queen next to her is tall and slender Channing LaRue. She's been doing drag for almost seven years. Several years ago she was a theater and music student named Andy at Carnegie Mellon University in Pittsburgh. Andy became a music teacher during his coming-out period in 1997. He soon quit teaching and began bartending, and now he is a hairdresser. Tonight as Channing, she describes drag as her "Aha!" moment. She had always wanted to perform, and within a year was doing drag one or two nights a week. She tells me her character, Channing, is a senator's wife with a background in ice skating.

The girls banter and joke while getting ready in the dressing room. It's an easy, relaxed atmosphere. The last of the performers, a sassy, dark-skinned Milano queen, named Iman Mykales, shows up shortly before showtime. She complains she got lost on the way from Kansas City, Mo. Iman makes her living on drag shows, doing four to five shows a week. She holds 11 titles, and is the reigning Miss Gay Kansas City, she says. She started 10 years ago, as Michael, on a bet from her friends. "And then began the drama," she says.

Show and Tell

It's almost 11 p.m., and the crowd starts to pour in. It's mostly gay men, some lesbians and straight women, and a handful of straight men. "The heteros come because they've never seen this before, except on Ricki Lake," Alexus says. A few people sneak into the dressing room, and everybody is eager to meet and greet the queens. Their celebrity status is obvious. I expect to be asked to leave the dressing room, but the queens seem to have forgotten I'm there. Desiree walks out topless in pantyhose and a girdle and I can only think two things: yes, her breasts are real, and they're bigger than mine. Alexus is in a top and pantyhose. They're singing and dancing to "Hey Ya" by OutKast while putting on their finishing touches. They tease each other and gossip. Iman's recounting an episode from earlier that week. "And I was like, I will whoop your ass and then put you in drag," she says to Desiree and Channing. Montana wears an outfit just for mingling with the audience before the show. I ask her what she uses to stuff, and she pulls a prosthetic breast covered in fabric out of her bra.

I take my place next to the catwalk. Alexus comes out from backstage in a black bustier and pants with one sequined-denim leg and the other rainbow-colored fringe. She also wears a blonde, shoulder-length wig. The buxom queen is the undisputed star of the show. People push to the front of the catwalk for a chance to put dollar bills in her top. Alexus also emcees the show, heckling the audience more than they heckle back. The show is a cross between a lip-synched concert, a beauty pageant, a pole-dancing show and a comedy club. Alexus announces Desiree, who shocks the audience in a fluorescent, multi-colored cat suit and neon yellow pigtails.

Next is Montana, donning a black leather jacket, black

sequined bustier and faded jeans. She has long silver talons and stilettos. She looks a bit like Madonna, with a Farrah Fawcett-inspired feathered mane. Alexus changes backstage into a slinky black dress with a hot pink shawl around her waist, and short brunette hair. She introduces Channing, about whom she jokes is just back from the Republican National Convention. Channing comes out in a bright green can-can dress and a long, blond feathered wig. During her routine, she strips to a neon orange and green ice-skating dress with sequins, and then twirls down to an even skimpier neon yellow fringed skating dress.

Alexus portrays Iman as a bad girl. "She's foul and she will cut you," Alexus warns the audience. Iman walks on stage in jeans, a sleeveless denim zippered top and plenty of bling-bling. The first half of the show wraps up with a slow song from Desiree to "I Believe in Miracles," by Whitney Houston. She's in an off-the-shoulder evening gown and adorned with fist-sized sparkling earrings.

At intermission, in the dressing room, I'm surprised to see Channing out of costume. I had almost forgotten the performers were men. Desiree is shaking her Tina Turner wig, making sure it's secure. The mood is subdued; the girls are getting into their next outfits, or silently rehearsing. They help each other get into costume and fix their hair. The quiet lasts only as long as intermission.

Iman starts the second half a seductive dance to "T-Shirt and My Panties On," by Adina Howard. She wears flashing jewelry that light up, a red body suit with red boots, a blue ripped T-shirt and a high ponytail that makes her resemble Naomi Campbell. The most important aspect of the show is the interaction with the audience. Alexus doesn't speak over the crowd, but rather to them, asking questions and commenting on select patrons' clothing or sexuality.

No one seems to mind even the harshest teasing. One girl is yelling Alexus' name, but Alexus can't see her. She yells back, "Are you pretty?" And then after a moment, "No, you're not because nobody said anything." After Montana's rendition of "Walking on Sunshine" in a yellow and pink swimsuit and leather jacket, Alexus announces Rock the Vote voter registration. She's not campaigning for Kerry as much as she's calling for the ousting of Bush. Next is Channing in another ice-skating outfit, this one blue. Her eyelids are heavily glittered and her routine includes an exhausting number of back kicks and twirls. The event everyone seems to have been waiting for is the pole-dancing competition. Young topless men are picked from the crowd. They strut down the catwalk and dance on the pole while the audience cheers and boos to vote for its favorite. One contestant reveals he's not wearing any underwear to the delight of the crowd. The show is winding down as Desiree, dressed as Tina Turner, performs an ambitious "Proud Mary." Out of breath, she announces Alexus, and the audience once again crowds the stage. In a white, sleek asymmetrical dress, Alexus ends the show with a fast-paced finale.

The queens and their entourages gather their costumes and makeup in the dressing room, while several fans come back to congratulate them on their show. I ask how long it will take to get out of drag, and they all tell me fewer than 20 minutes. "I like to put it on, but I love to take it off," Montana says After almost eight hours at the show, I wonder how these provocative performers can do this night after night. I slip out quietly, knowing it will be a long time before the girls will get past their fans.

Know your vocab

Drag Queen/King: A person, usually homosexual, who dresses in exaggerated clothing and makeup of the opposite sex. Drag is a form of performing art.

Cross-Dresser: A person, usually heterosexual, who dresses in clothing of the opposite sex, sometimes as a sexual fetish.

Transsexual: A person who switches sex through hormones, surgery or both.

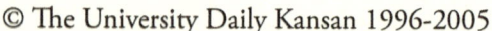

Consumer Magazine Article: Investigation & Analysis

the face of AIDS in africa

Joanna Mayhew, Boston University

Shifting the Shame

"The culture is promoting AIDS; no question about it," Susan Aradeon, Ph.D. said, shaking her head. "As long as the norm is multiple partners, there will be AIDS."

For this reason, Aradeon, Senior Behavior Change Communication Specialist for the Benin Integrated Family Health Project (PROSAF), lists "promoting contraception to prevent multiple partners" as one of her organization's main objectives in Benin.

PROSAF, a contractor for USAID, was created in 1999 and is located in the Borgou-Alibori Department of Benin. In the year 2000, the department had an AIDS prevalence rate of eight percent – two times the estimated percentage for the country. Still – "I don't know why it's not higher; I don't believe it's not higher," admitted Aradeon, revealing a slight northeastern-American accent. The most probable reason it is not higher is that, in the past, commercial sex workers did not frequent Benin because there was no money in the country. And by the time these workers came, Population Services International (PSI) had widely promoted condoms, according to Aradeon. So, ironically, Benin has potentially benefited by being a poor country.

One part, about a fifth, of the PROSAF project is behavior change. This section, Aradeon's, has its work cut out for it. The Beninese culture not only has deep-seated traditions and norms, but it also a communal culture. Therefore, in order to change the mindsets of individuals, PROSAF first has to change the beliefs of groups.

"We promote family planning to keep the man inside the house," said Aradeon, swiveling in her roller chair to face me. Her office was airy and quiet – everyone else had left for the day. "We're promoting contraception so that the husband doesn't go to other women."

The Beninese believe that a man should not have relations with his wife from the time she is showing in pregnancy until the baby is grown. Traditionally, people thought sperm would kill the unborn baby, said Aradeon. Each ethnic group has a different length of time that should be adhered to after birth. The longest is among the Yoruba – they believe the couple should not have sex until the baby is three-years-old. Islam states that the couple should wait for two years, except to consummate the birth at 42 days after delivery.

Historically, women also returned to their families when pregnant, and this is still frequently practiced. They often stay there until the baby is old enough to come off their back, or about two years.

"People here believe a man physically has to have lots of sex," said Aradeon, as we walked outside past a row of shiny PROSAF SUV vehicles to her car. The setting sun was painting the sky a mélange of rusty colors. "The women believe it too," she continued as she drove. If both believe it, and a man's wife is often gone for up to two years, the result seems obvious. "He's going to have multiple partners. People have to use condoms."

A few moments later, a loud "Shit!" erupted out of Aradeon's mouth. With all dashboard warning signs blinking, her car had lurched to a stop – approximately 10 feet outside of her gate. As it was almost dark outside, she placed orange triangular warning signs behind and in front of her car. "Life is never too easy," she said with an exasperated sigh as we walked into the house.

And as for the consideration of men waiting without sex for their wives to have the baby – "They don't believe it. They think it's unacceptable to assume a grown man can stop from having sex."

Aradeon knows what she is talking about. Though she has only lived in Benin for three years, she spent 25 years in Nigeria and is married to a Nigerian. "That's why I know so much about the culture – I'm right," Aradeon said, in a matter-of-fact tone that strangely gave no hint of conceit. "I say things others aren't saying."

Abstinence does result from these "after birth" traditions, but in a different sense. Abstinence within the marriage takes place – the abstinence that exists when a man is running around with other women. And as the object of getting married in Benin is to have children, a couple gets pregnant as soon as they tie the knot. Therefore, a couple begins being "abstinent" right at the start of their marriage.

PROSAF promotes contraception to solve this problem – so that a husband can continue having sex with his own wife without inevitable pregnancy. This promotion comes in various forms – ranging from theatrical plays to radio spots to interactive sessions on AIDS. In each medium, PROSAF pushes condoms, as well as other contraceptives, over abstinence.

"We've done a lot of promotion of condoms," said Aradeon, disappearing into her bedroom momentarily. I glanced around the large living room. The tidy white-tiled area was comfortably sparse – decorated only by a couch set, coffee table, chandelier light, and blank white walls. "Couples have to start using them when the epidemic is really bad in a country," she said, in a loud voice that traveled through the empty room. "They won't use them if they have a bad rap. We want to normalize them so people will use them."

PSI has been trying to "normalize" condoms for some years by promoting them through radio and television. Religious groups often make the accusation that people haven't been sensitized enough to abstinence, but they are not using these media, according to Aradeon.

"Mass media works," said Aradeon as she emerged from the bedroom. She had changed from her business skirt and blouse to a typical simple Beninese dress – a colorful, cool, and comfortable one-piece that falls like a nightgown. Her gray hair was elegantly swept up into a tight bun.

PROSAF airs various messages through many rural radio stations, as well as in Parakou. These messages air in all different languages – French, Bariba, Fulani, Dendi. "If you want to reach people, radio spots are very important; they get information out – but they don't change attitudes."

Abstinence wouldn't work because asking a Beninese man to abstain is like asking him to be "effeminate," said Aradeon. It seems completely abnormal not to "satisfy." For the young people, PROSAF encourages them to "delay" until they have a partner rather than "abstain."

"Delay doesn't mean sex is bad – abstinence does."

And faithfulness? "Fidelity isn't a product, it's an attitude. People have never heard of it." For this reason, fidelity wouldn't have been successful even if promoted over the media, said Aradeon.

"It's unrealistic to ask people to be faithful. The key is to reduce the number of partners," she paused before dejectedly adding, "But they don't understand that."

I asked Aradeon what she thought about a sight that

had often bothered me in Parakou. At the entrance to the city, a big Prudence-brand condoms sign boasts "l'amour sans risque," love without risk. But, having grown up in the United States, I knew that there was still a risk – maybe small – with using condoms.

"It's better to tell people it's without risk than to say that condoms are 'without risk, except in the case of such and such,'" replied Aradeon, just as the room was enveloped in darkness – the electricity had been cut. I had become accustomed to these frequent cuts soon after moving to Parakou. Aradeon had adapted to them, as well – she continued talking as if nothing had happened. "Public-health wise, you are protecting them much more by pushing condoms."

Very few condoms break; millions are used without breaking. We only hear about the few that do, according to Aradeon. As far as contraceptives being dangerous, childbirth creates a much higher risk. "And contraceptives are a choice." We choose to get in the car when there is a bigger risk in that, she reasoned.

"I think it's a moral imperative to advise them that it is without risk," Aradeon stated firmly. With that, she finally made a move toward a light. She carried in two bright fluorescent lamps that accentuated the whiteness of the room.

PROSAF has organized various plays, in French and Bariba, advocating condoms. One, titled "Spacing our Children," toured for eight months starting in September of 2000. Another, "Condoms for Prevention of AIDS," was performed along with a "pre-test" and a "post-test." PROSAF discovered that before the play, 50 percent of the audience knew condoms can prevent AIDS and 25 percent considered loyalty or abstinence. After the play, 100 percent understood condoms can prevent the disease and 75 percent considered loyalty or abstinence. The play also emphasizes "parent-to-child" transmission rather than simply mother-to-child transmission. PROSAF wants people to understand that fathers can give it to their children by first giving it to their wives. "Hopefully that'll make them think," said Aradeon, getting up and motioning me towards the raised dining room.

The organization also runs other plays that try to reduce the fear and stigma of those living with AIDS. For example, in one called "Fighting AIDS," which recently finished touring in secondary schools, the actors are portrayed as eating out of the same bowl as those who are HIV-positive – without getting infected by them.

Aradeon hopes to soon begin a new phase of awareness – through interactive sessions in various villages. The information content would include discussions on AIDS, human sexuality, human sexual response, traditional norms they have retained, sexual norms that are being passed down, whether these norms are positive or harmful, and whether it is desirable to pass the same norms down to the next generation or to change them.

She originally had the vision for these groups because she saw the young actors from the plays change their mindsets towards sex. Why? "They were immersed by the information."

Therefore, the setup for these sessions will be four groups of 15 to 20 people who get together twice a week. They will have 15 meetings of two-and-a-half hours each – the equivalent of a six-day workshop. Aradeon wants them to absorb the information and share it with others.

PROSAF does not aim their radio broadcasts, plays, and interactive sessions at a single group of people in the population. "There is an underlying belief that if you don't change the men's mindsets, you can forget it," she said. "But it takes two to tango."

As far as "peer educators" in schools, Aradeon thinks the concept is ridiculous. "Twenty kids trying to change the minds of 2000? Bull shit! It won't work."

PROSAF does have an ultimate focus as far as education, though. They want people to know two methods of contraception and two symptoms of STDs for their own sex.

"We're trying to get the community to change something," said Aradeon, passing me a big bowl of sticky rice and vegetables.

'Trying to get the community to is exactly what PROSAF is up against – the community. Collectivism dominates Beninese culture – "It's pervasive," said Aradeon, in between mouthfuls. "It's very hard to change if people don't want you to. People in Benin are raised to respond to collective pressure."

When you ask men to reduce their number of partners or use contraception, you are asking them to change a behavior that is linked to their identity.

"Look at the goddamn map!" interjected Susan suddenly, with her fork raised in the air. I gave her a questioning look, and she clarified. "AIDS started in the States!" In the 1970s and 1980s, AIDS blossomed in the gay community and spread throughout cocaine circles. "But it didn't spread into the middle class. Why not?"

I responded to her question with a second puzzled look.

"Because men having multiple partners after marriage is not at the core of their identity in the States," said Aradeon. American men are not placing their social relationships at risk, not diminishing themselves, by not chasing other women. In Benin, to some extent, men are.

Pressure exists for women, as well. When a married Bariba woman returns to her home town for a ceremony or other special event, she is devalued if no man is "interested" in her.

"It's not easy. People have to choose between a health risk and a social risk. The two are in conflict; you can't have it both ways," said Aradeon, wiping the sweat from her forehead. With the electricity still non-existent, the heat was stifling. "And in a collective society, it's very hard to put your identity at risk." Therefore, PROSAF aims to change people's collective behavior rather than their individual behavior.

The choice between a health risk and a social risk is further simplified by the fact that the Beninese people do not understand the AIDS disease.

"We believe the science in our bodies without question," said Aradeon. Raised an atheist in a New Jersey suburb of NYC, she had no science in high school. But, everything she knows about science she has always believed "on faith" of her society, regardless of never learning it herself.

People in Benin believe in sorcery or fetishes for the same reason – their society does. They don't understand science and viruses, said Aradeon.

"And the AIDS virus is a smarter-than-hell virus. It survives by hiding." AIDS can even hide for up to ten years before ever rearing its ugly head.

"But we can understand a disease hiding in a body; people here can't." Aradeon paused as her "home help," a shy girl of about 18, appeared to clear our plates and serve dessert – mangos. As they were in-season, mangos had become a staple food for me. I didn't know how I would ever part with them in a few months. I eagerly dived into the fruit as she continued, "Even the well-educated have a hard time comprehending."

Benin's collectivist society is in transition. The former society had many more social controls, but now taxation, education, jobs and consumer goods are all individualized. These are all causing a breakdown in the traditional power of elderly people in the villages, said Aradeon.

However, people are leaving old communal pressures only to find new ones away from their village. "Fundamentalism wins – replacing old control with new control." The victory of fundamentalism is obvious in the rapid growth of structured religions like Islam in Benin – where their lifestyle is decided for them.

"They don't grow up making decisions; decisions are made for them by family and community." I nodded my agreement – testimony of my time here – and filled my glass with water for the sixth time. It was a vain attempt to make up for all the fluid I was losing to perspiration. "They find security in clear decisions; we find it in choice," she added.

Westerners are brought up to confront everything in front of them. The Beninese, on the other hand, are taught not to question anything society tells them, said Aradeon.

The collectivist society in Benin also brings with it a different moral control system. The system is regulated by fear – of what would happen to you if do something wrong – but more dominantly by shame – that you would be spurned by society and bring shame on yourself and your family if you do wrong.

The "glory and shame" culture had puzzled me since I had arrived in Benin. I had seen it played out in numerous different scenarios throughout my short time in the country. The culture programs people to first and foremost do anything to bring glory to themselves; and secondly, if not equally as important as the first, to avoid doing anything that will bring shame on themselves.

The shame aspect is confusing because shame is not brought on a person by a wrongdoing; shame is only brought when the person's wrongdoing is discovered.

In the West, people feel guilt for doing something wrong. "Very different," Aradeon stated simply.

An example of this is if somebody brings new jeans for everyone in their village. That person will receive glory for the deed, even if everyone suspects the person stole the jeans. However, if it is found out that the goods were stolen, then the act is wrong and that person is shamed – but not until the act is uncovered.

The same holds true along the line of AIDS. A majority of the population is sleeping around, whether married or unmarried – and, under the surface, everyone knows it. But, if it is disclosed that a person has AIDS, that person is shamed – because his or her promiscuity has been revealed.

Though I had often found this culture, which is so different from the West, confusing and therefore frustrating, Aradeon was more positive. "I'm trying to use it. It's not the way I was brought up," she said, holding out the palm of her hand to concede the fact. "But there's good in it."

Aradeon, through PROSAF, is trying to change how and why people are morally sanctioned. She wants to change what people are shamed by – for example, change the shame of being HIV-positive to the shame of having unprotected sex.

"That's exactly what we're trying do – shift the shame." Aradeon wants to establish "shame sanctions" for people who do things that are negative health-wise and "praise sanctions" on those who have positive habits.

This same strategy would be used with family planning. Instead of a man being shamed by having few children, as is tradition, the man would be shamed by having too many kids to bring them all up correctly, she said.

Aradeon has had these ideas for behavioral change since 1992. "I knew the culture," she repeated. She began working for USAID in 1993 – or more specifically for PATH, Program for Appropriate Technology and Health, under which she is currently employed while working on the PROSAF project. She had no formal training in behavior communication before being signed on with USAID. "I just read everything." With an unpretentious grin, she added, "If you have a Ph.D., you know how to read."

Aradeon had a myriad of jobs before joining USAID – ranging from a Peace Corps teacher to a BCC officer in the Pacific to a university professor of archeological history. "I'm a career changer," she said, shrugging her shoulders with a smile. Though involved elsewhere, she had always wanted to do something with behavior communication. "And now I'm doing it," she said, staring past my shoulder. "I'm really lucky."

Her eyes quickly snapped back into focus as she returned to her shame-shifting idea. "So that's what I'm trying to do. We have to change what's a 'good person' – but it's too hard to do as individuals."

The goal of changing groups of people at a time was hard for me to understand. As a Westerner, I have heard the phrase, "One person at a time," said innumerable times – as a kind of idealistic way of reasoning that you can't change the world overnight, but every person and every step towards the goal counts. I realized I had no idea how you would realistically go about changing the minds of groups. So I asked Aradeon.

"To be honest, I don't think we know very well. My personal aim is to try to find better ways."

The dramas work well with groups because people see everyone else react. People see that others have the same misconceptions as them. Take the play where the people are eating out of same bowl as AIDS victims – people realize that others thought it was possible to catch the disease through that, too.

In the West, there is a mindset that people need to talk about things – bring them into the open – for change to occur. So Western agencies often try to use that same method in Benin. "But people here can't talk about sex. People will start talking about contraceptives after they are all using them – not before." Through the dramas, people can learn together without being in a threatening atmosphere, said Aradeon.

Aradeon's outlook for the future is mixed. She began by saying, "If I'm honest, it's hopeless. Because family planning is the core of identity – and, historically, to have successful family is to have lots of kids."

But this idea is fading, she later said. Beninese society is in transition. Ten years ago in Benin, sex meant placing sperm inside a woman. Now, people do not hold to that belief. Instead, they are starting to think condoms are a good idea – though she added that of course they do not always use them. They may not, but the statistics are positive. In the Borgou-Alibori Department, the 1996 statistics showed that less than six percent of people used contraceptives. In 2002, there was 11 percent contraceptive use, and the numbers are even higher now. The tradition of after-birth abstinence has also broken down quite a bit.

"It takes time to change these ideas," said Aradeon. She believes change happens in about a half generation

– a 25 year-old mother passes on new information to her niece, rather than her daughter.

"But if you are waiting 10 years for change with AIDS, the epidemic is getting deeper and deeper into society."

Aradeon does not believe, as others I had met did, that people need to know somebody with AIDS in order to change. "If they did, I'd give up."

But, she admits people need to know "a lot." They need to know they are at risk with multiple partners. And, if they want to be faithful in marriage, both members of the couple have to make that choice – and even then there is a personal risk.

"With the sexual practices, though, there is no reason to think that AIDS won't escalate – rapidly."

Her confusing responses were more confirmation to me of the complexity of AIDS – and that there is no clear answer for the future of Benin.

Aradeon adjusted her thin glasses and glanced anxiously around the room. "What time is it?" The lack of electricity always makes it seem later than it is – but we had been talking for a while. It was already past 10. Not wanting me to walk in the dark, and having no functioning car to drive me home, Aradeon offered to let me spend the night.

I thanked her for her generous offer but declined it. As I gathered my things, Aradeon continued, saying, "Too often, you don't respect the people you're trying to change. You have to respect them. Why should everyone have to live like you?" She chuckled quietly before adding, "In our case, because they'll live better!"

She walked me to the door of her circular house. "And there are too few people involved in AIDS work who really understand the local culture – so it's a great opportunity."

We paused in front of her small gazebo as she called

for the young girl who had served us dinner. Aradeon insisted that she walk me to the road, where I could find a motorcycle taxi. I stared up at the sky as we waited. The clarity of the innumerable stars made me immensely grateful for the power cut.

"I love my work, no question about it," said Aradeon softly, next to me in the darkness. "Who could ask for a better job?"

Acquiesce

"Your sickness is common in the country right now," the long unnerving silence that followed the statement was finally broken by, "The sickness is called SIDA."

The gravity of what I was witnessing hit me like a punch in the gut. I was sitting in the back of a small bare classroom as Martha Koetsier told her newest patient, Esther, that she was HIV-positive. I could only see the woman's left side. Esther was a beautiful lady who looked about 25 but was actually over 40. She had two traditional Bariba scars – a semicircle curving in towards her mouth on each cheek. She wore a green-and-black light nylon scarf over her head and yellow flip-flops a size too small.

As I watched the consultation, I couldn't help feeling guilty that I knew exactly what sicknesses and social rejection Martha's last statement implied, and that Esther did not. As Paul, a local co-worker of about 24, translated Martha's French into Bariba, Esther's face remained unchanged. She kept her soft brown eyes focused on him and nodded with a "Toh," meaning okay.

Martha locked her concerned aqua blue eyes, accentuated by her blue-beaded necklace and blue dress, on Esther with a clenched jaw as she asked, "Do you know of the sickness?"

"C'est la mort," Esther bluntly replied in French – It's the death.

Esther did not know the details of AIDS – how it's contracted, what it does to a person's immune system, how far-spread its impact is in the world – but she knew the bottom line. It would kill her.

As much ignorance as there is in Benin surrounding AIDS, Martha usually finds that people are at least aware of the fact of looming death.

Even as she spoke the morbid words, Esther remained unsurprised and unperturbed. She shed no tears and raised no objection. She simply accepted her fate.

I felt like jumping up in her place; I wanted to argue for her, "But how? Why? This isn't fair! I had plans for my future! This can't be happening to me!" But I sat still in the uncomfortable child-size chair and tried to swallow her resignation.

Esther's blood had been tested the day before at HEB, Evangelical Hospital of Bembereke, the governmental zone hospital in the town of Bembereke, in the northern half of Benin. HEB is considered one of the best hospitals in the country, and Martha's AIDS counseling and awareness project is a branch off of the hospital. Esther had come to seek help at HEB because she had been struggling with a variety of problems for over two years – periodic diarrhea, weight loss, body aches, and sores in her mouth and vagina.

Martha had started this meeting in her temporary schoolroom office with the test results. "Yesterday we tested your blood and found a little problem. It's a little complicated so we invited you here to explain." Martha now follows this protocol about 10 times a month – the rate at which she is receiving new patients.

She had then gone on to ask Esther some background questions – age, family situation, occupation. Esther didn't know how old she is but had already had 10 children, three of whom died. The youngest is eight. As most HIV-positive children die before the age of five, her little ones are safe. She lives in N'Dali, a town about 45 minutes away, at her brother's house. As there are no house numbers or street names in Benin, Martha took about 20 minutes to get an idea of exactly where the house is in order to follow-up on Esther. For a living, Esther sells pounded yams, a staple food for every Beninese. She is married, but her husband lives in Banikoara, about four hours north of N'Dali.

Separation during marriage is a norm in Benin. A wife only stays with her husband for certain periods of time. Once a woman is pregnant she will often go back to her family until the baby is finished nursing. A woman will also return to her family when she begins menopause – because men believe that if they sleep with a post-menopausal women they will get "a disease." And, as in Esther's case, a woman will return to her family when she is sick. Esther told Martha she plans to stay with her family.

This division in the home usually leads the husband to find other women – Esther's husband had two other wives, but she was the first. Bariba culture names the second wife "Nissi," which literally translated means "jealousy."

"Now I'm going to explain the sickness you have," continued Martha after gaining little solid information from Esther. "We found you have a little germ. This germ is a little complicated; it causes you to stay sick for a long time." She went on to explain that Esther's white blood cells are not able to fight against the sickness; that they no longer have a defense against the sickness.

As Paul translated to Esther, I wondered if she even understood the term "white blood cells" – the type of knowledge I took for granted. I was later told by Martha that Paul does not translate her literally when it comes to explaining AIDS. He has worked for her long enough that he understands what she wants to communicate, but he is also Bariba and knows how to put it in terms that his people understand. "He just does it in a way that she'll get the point," Martha told me.

This was the moment Martha had hit Esther with the word "SIDA."

After Esther's acquiesce to imminent death, I anxiously wondered where Martha would launch. The beating fan above seemed deafening. She went with a positive route – if that was possible, considering the circumstances.

"There are medicines to help you with this sickness, but not to cure it. However, this doesn't mean you will die tomorrow. We can help fight the sickness."

Martha went on to explain that Esther would have to take an antibiotic – Bactrim – every day for the rest of her life. She said that these tablets would increase her resistance against easily getting infections. She added that, if it were okay, they would like to stop by her home from time to time to check on her. Martha told me that these home visits not only speak value into people's lives but also help her to know what kind of situation they live in – how much money they have and how many people they have to help care for them.

"There are things that you can do to help yourself, too," Martha continued, with a comforting smile. She explained the necessity of changing her eating habits a little bit – basic routines that any Westerner would have been taught from a young age. She told her she must cook her food well before eating, or else she will get bad diarrhea; if she eats uncooked food, she must clean it well before eating. She should fill her diet with vegetables, fruits, beef, and eggs.

She must also sleep with a mosquito net. And, if she gets a small infection or cut, she must take care of it quickly. Martha slowly explained that usually small problems like this would go away within a week, but for her, now, it could become a big problem if not treated.

Martha then moved on to a more sensitive subject — sex.

"The disease usually comes when two people are sexually involved," she said, "I don't know how you got it, but it is possible the other people involved have it." Martha later told me that she rarely tries to discover exactly how a person contracted SIDA. "It doesn't concern me now. The person could have been infected for eight or nine years already."

With Esther sitting expressionless, Martha continued. "If you sleep with other people you could infect them, too. Does your husband come to visit often?"

"No," Esther slowly shook her head.

I thought of her husband's two other wives. I wondered how many children they both had. AIDS could have already infected a half dozen people in this one family.

"It's necessary to check if he has it. The only was to find out is to look at the blood. He could have the disease for a long time before becoming sick. You have to tell him that you have a disease that he might also have."

Esther spoke softly, for the first time in minutes. "I don't have enough energy to go."

Martha urged that it was important for somebody to take a message to him. "I don't know if that will happen,"

Martha confided to me later. She told Esther that her disease not only concerned her, but also concerned her whole family.

"It's often that if one person in the couple has it, the others will have it." Martha had a simple yet truthful way of putting things.

Pen in hand, she asked Esther for the name of her husband and his location in Banikoara. Esther said his name was Zachary, but she didn't know his last name. Sadly, this could either be true or false. Either she had ten children by a man she only knew by first name, or she was trying to protect him from shame.

Martha closed her session by emphasizing that Esther must take her medicine each day. She told me that most people take the medicine until they start to feel better. Then they assume they are cured and quit the medicine, only to have their sicknesses come back with a vengeance. "You will be tired a lot; you will not have good health."

She told Esther not to spend her money on Fetish healers, but instead to spend it on good food. Money management is a tough subject to teach in Africa. Culture in Benin does not allow much room for saving. If you have any money, your family and friends expect to have access to it – either to borrow or take. Nothing stays in one hand for more than a few days.

Martha asked Esther if she had any questions. The elegant statue swept her eyes downward to signal a "no."

"Do you have diarrhea now?"

"Not now, but I recently had it for a month."

"So, it's already begun," Martha muttered dejectedly to me in English.

Esther was told to come back in the month. For the medication, testing, and consultation, Esther had to pay

5,000 CFA – about 10 US dollars. Each successive visit would only cost her 1,000 CFA, just enough to cover the medicine.

As they got up to leave, Esther let out another "Toh." She shyly smiled at Martha and gave a half curtsey as she said, "Ka somburu" meaning, "Good work."

Mystified, I watched her carefully walk out the door and up the dirt path. A slim, dark silhouette against a blinding sun-lit landscape; a woman unmoved by the fact that her world had just shifted beneath her.

The Whole World Mourns

I gritted my teeth and tried to ignore the smell as I removed the soiled diaper. The odor was so overpowering it dominated the large cement living room of the orphanage. This job was pushing my limit. At home, I would at least have the clean comfort of disposable Luvs diapers and wet wipes. Not in Africa. Cloth diapers for the babies and panties for the toddlers – both washed by hand. During the day, most would go without either, leaving their presents on the floor.

Though a Canadian runs the orphanage, Margaret Bevington, who has been there since 1957, she wisely keeps it a little "Africanized." If the children get used to complete cleanliness and are then taken in by a bush family, they will no longer have resistance against diseases easily picked up on the dirt floors.

I was changing Boni, the youngest baby in the orphanage, before laying him down for a nap. He was lucky he was so darn cute – milk chocolate complexion, toothless smile, pudgy arms and legs, and a little Afro on top. If not, he might have gone out the window along with his stinky diaper.

I spent about 10 minutes trying to decipher how to get the new diaper on – the material, safety pins, and nylon lining much too large and awkward for his little bottom. After deciding that it wouldn't completely slide off, I carried him over to throw his old diaper into the designated bucket, dreading dealing with it later.

I picked up a few toys and put them back on my way to Boni's bed. By the time we reached it, I regrettably discovered that he was wet again. I headed back to the "changing area" – namely whatever free chair I could find. No sooner had I gotten the next diaper clipped on than Boni went to the toilet again. Three diapers in less than three minutes. Unbelievable. Definitely just to test my patience. I shook my head at Boni, and he responded with his usual laugh – mouth fully open and sounds coming out, but no movement. I couldn't help but laugh at the adorable way he mocked my situation.

When I finally laid him down in his small rickety wood crib – dry for the time being – I heard a line I had heard numerous times over the past couple months. "Make sure you peg the mosquito net down tight. Cover all the corners." Margaret was completely overprotective of Boni. He had separate diapers, towels, blankets, milk, water, and food from the rest of the children. She had a hard time letting me do anything for him; she wanted to be sure everything was done her way.

I couldn't blame her, though. Boni had been premature – born seven months into his mother's pregnancy. She hadn't made it through the delivery; so Boni had been dropped off by the family at the orphanage. He had been on the verge of death when he arrived at Margaret's door – just skin and bones. She had spent weeks feeding him through an eyedropper around the clock.

He had now been at the orphanage for six months and had made outstanding progress. He had rounded out and was now a completely healthy and cheerful baby. He also seemed to be Margaret's favorite, but she would never admit to it.

When I arrived at Margaret's the next week, after fighting my way through her petting zoo of 8 goats and 12 chickens outside, I was shocked to find Boni gone. As I heated water for morning baths, I asked Margaret where he had gone. She seemed busy moving things around the kitchen crowded with baby bottles and laundry and said, "Oh, yes, Boni's gone." For the second time, I asked where. "Oh, his family came and took him."

"They did?" I said, surprised. I hadn't heard any news of this beforehand. "Was that expected?"

"No." Margaret didn't seem to want to talk.

As I watched the kettle boil, I was suddenly filled with sadness. I realized that in my short time in the orphanage, Boni had managed to worm his way to the center of my heart. I was happy that he was home, but upset that I hadn't been able to say goodbye. I also knew that nowhere else in the world could offer love and care like Margaret could.

I thought of Margaret, who had saved his life and been a mother to him since birth. "How do you do that?" I asked, amazed by her. "How do you raise them and then just let them go?" Margaret, always unaffected and tough after 46 years of doing this, replied with "You just do. You have to."

"But how do you keep them without becoming attached?" Margaret gave the first half-smile of the morning, revealing the deep wrinkles surrounding her glistening brown eyes, as she responded, "Well, that's impossible."

Still seemingly distracted, she left the room and me with my thoughts. I couldn't imagine having her life. The job of raising these children would be hard enough in itself, but to then entrust them to a new family or back to their own family...I would never last in her profession.

One week later, I returned home after another morning of dodging urine puddles, serving bouille, and playing peek-a-boo with the kids. I paid my motorbike-taxi driver, thankful to just be alive after the way he had torn through the city. I was preparing a salad as Mary, my co-worker and next-door neighbor, stopped in to say hello.

She kindly asked me how the kids were and how my morning had gone. I sadly told her it was much quieter – I had said goodbye to another baby, Waru, who had been picked up by his new family.

"Did Margaret ever tell you the truth about the little one?" She asked, hesitatingly.

"What do you mean? Who? Boni?" I asked, confused. At an affirmative nod, I fumbled with words, "Well, yeah, she told me his family came to get him..." I trailed off as I saw her look down and away. I suddenly felt dread clutch my chest. "No way," I shook my head emphatically. "Don't tell me...don't tell me...he died?" My pleading was to no avail; she nodded affirmatively.

"I'm sorry, Joanna. He died a week and a half ago. I thought she must have told you by now."

My heart seemed to stop at the words ringing in my ears. I looked down as my eyes filled with tears, blurring the tomatoes I was chopping into a wavy sea of red. It couldn't be true; I must have heard wrong.

"But how?" My voice cracked at the words. I wasn't sure if I wanted to hear anything, but it was worse not knowing. "Why didn't she tell me?"

"She knew how attached you already were to him. She thought it would be too much for you…" She spoke cautiously, as if tiptoeing on thin ice. "I'm sorry to just throw that on you. But I thought you needed to know the truth…"

Anything else she said flew past me. As she turned to go, I wearily thanked her for telling me; that it was better I knew.

I sat through lunch like a zombie; then sat through work useless. My mind was consumed with little Boni. And with questions. How did he die? Why? Had he been sick for a long time?

Whether Margaret had wanted me to know or not, now I did. I needed to see her.

When I reached the small blue-framed house, I found her parked outside in her rusty red 1970s station wagon. She had loaded up all the kids in the back and was headed for the market. At 71-years-old, she was still too independent to let anyone else do her shopping for her. She invited me into the front seat and poured herself some water out of an old dust-covered Coke bottle.

Surprised to see me, she bluntly asked why I had come. Margaret wastes no time. Not knowing how to bring the painful subject up, I explained to her that I was going to be away that coming weekend and wouldn't be able to make it that Friday to help.

"You didn't have to come all this way to tell me that. You could have just called."

Right. Good point. With no way out, I launched.

"Well, actually, I, uh, wanted to talk to you about something," I said slowly, knowing I was on the verge of tears for the fiftieth time that day. She gave me a nudging 'get on with it' look.

"I know about Boni. Mary told me. And, I just, uh, I just wanted you to know that I know." I let my elegant statement rest at that.

Margaret let out a long sigh. "Poor Boni."

With those two words, she promptly turned her head to look outside the window. She did her best to hide from everyone, but I could see her cheeks start to wobble. Soon tears found their way down to her chin. I was completely taken back. The toughest lady I have ever met was now broken before me.

My heavy heart went out to her. "I wish you would have told me. I understand you had good intentions, but I wouldn't be in Benin if I wanted to protect myself from this type of..."

"It's too hard," she said, interrupting and trying unsuccessfully to gain composure. "When little babies die like that, it's too hard for me to talk about it." Suddenly it made sense. It wasn't for my sake that she withheld the news of Boni's death; it was for hers. She couldn't bring herself to speak the heartrending words. "And his family did come for him," she said, trying to justify herself, "They came for the body."

I asked how it happened, knowing it was hard for her but also knowing I needed answers.

"Had he been sick?" I asked, trying to start somewhere.

"No," she said, frustrated, "He wasn't sick at all." She painfully recounted what had happened, interrupted periodically by kids in the back asking irrelevant questions, tugging at her silvery hair, or reaching for water.

Boni hadn't had any signs of sickness. "Perfectly healthy." Ten days ago she had put him down for a nap, but he had carried on crying. She had picked him up just in time to see his eyes roll back and his body flop unconscious. She had tried to take him to the dispensary, but her unreliable Renault 4 had a flat tire. She had quickly begged a neighbor to take them. But, after arriving at the nearest government dispensary, they had been told that nothing could be done for Boni.

I interrupted. "What do you mean, nothing could be done?" I asked incredulously.

Well, for some unknown reason, the dispensary did not have any medicine that day. I asked if this happened regularly and was told it does.

So, the nurses had sent the dying baby on his way. Margaret had then rushed him to the next-closest dispensary. Before anyone there was available to see them, Boni was gone.

Margaret had no more to say. She looked drained. She had probably played those few hours over and over in her mind. I wiped away the tears that had been pouring quietly down my cheeks. She offered to drive me back. We rode in silence. I flatly thanked her at the end of the short trip and told her I'd see her the following week.

For the next few days, I felt as if my life had been thrown into a tailspin. I couldn't stop crying; I couldn't think of anything but poor Boni. It wasn't fair that his life was cut drastically short. He had been saved at birth; now for what purpose?

I was overwhelmed with an amount of sorrow I have never felt before. My chest seemed to carry one hundred tons of weight on it. I was heartbroken over Boni, but somehow I sensed it was bigger than him. I was crushed by the fact that this occurrence is so common here. Life is a gift quickly taken away from many in Benin. Children often die before the age of two for simple reasons – cold, flu, dehydration. It was as if I could suddenly feel all the suffering surrounding me. And I didn't know how to carry that load. I felt lost.

I spent time praying to and questioning God. Suffering in the world is one of the hardest things to comprehend. Why are innocent babies dying when all that would save them is a simple antibiotic?

I felt as if God was saying, "I'm letting you hear my heartbeat." He had a purpose for Boni's life, and He too is heartbroken by the tragic shortening of the joyful child's time on earth. He was allowing me, just for a time, to weep with Him – to feel His pain. I was struck by the verse, "Sorrow not as those without hope." (I Thess. 4:13) It didn't say not to sorrow; mourning was necessary. But because I knew that God's love outweighs all the confusion, there was still hope in the deepest darkest place of sadness.

Sages used to say that when one life is saved, the whole world rejoices. When one life is lost, the whole world mourns. They said this to illustrate that groups of people don't die – individuals do. And each one counts.

The infant mortality rate is almost 10 percent. But that didn't matter. Boni was not a statistic; he was a life. And he was dead. To me, his death represented every death.

The heaviness did not last forever; I slowly found my smile again. But, something has changed within me. No longer will I be able to hear of poverty-stricken people dying without pausing…and remembering. The whole world mourns. No matter who it was – regardless of race, religion, age or status – the world is not the same without that person.

The following Friday, I sat feeding one of the toddlers on the orphanage's cold gray floor. Sabi, about 17 months old, had been abandoned by his family for superstitious reasons. As I tried unsuccessfully to get him to eat rather than throw the chopped-up spaghetti, he reached his stick-like arms out towards me with a single word – "mama."

I realized I didn't understand Boni's death, and never would. But I knew one thing. Sabi and the others were still alive – and needed love.

I reached towards Sabi's outstretched arms and, as I picked him up out of a heap of stray noodles, hugged him close – wet bottom and all.

the withlacoochee: a river in balance

Sarah L. Stewart, University of Florida

The bird swoops low over the pontoon boat, offering passengers a fleeting head-on glimpse of beady eyes and a hooked bill. Captain Mike leans over the side of the boat, straining for a better look before it crosses the river and disappears into the cypress trees on the other side.

After consulting a worn field guide, he's pretty sure it was an immature Mississippi Kite. It's the first time he has seen this migratory bird in flight, he tells his passengers, his satisfaction audible as if marking a mental checklist. The boat hasn't yet left its cracked cement ramp, and already nature is showing off.

As Captain Mike Tracy, certified eco-tour guide, steers the 24-foot boat upstream at two or three miles an hour, he begins the story of the Withlacoochee River in his rich, showman's voice.

The Withlacoochee, or "little great river," gouged its path 17,000 years ago through primarily limestone beds. On its 157-mile northward journey through seven central Florida counties, it drops just 18 feet from its headwaters in the Green Swamp to a spot just north of Yankeetown where it empties into the Gulf of Mexico.

As he speaks, Captain Mike's brown eyes scan the river banks. He spots a turtle sunning on a branch just above water level, the first of many on today's route. The four passengers at the back of the boat, all of retirement age, leave their seats for a closer look. Turtles can only absorb sun through their skin, Captain Mike says, which explains why its head and legs are extended from the shell.

"They kinda look like Superman trying to fly," he says with a laugh.

The boat nears a spot where Captain Mike and his first trip of the day saw an alligator. He trains his binoculars on the bank, hoping to fulfill his passengers' requests to see Florida's most famous reptile.

"Well, he went hidin'," he says. "Little bugger." He sounds like he feels stood up.

"You little stinker. We'll have to find some other ones."

***

Beaches, rivers, lakes, swamps, springs. Second to sunshine, water is probably Florida's most sought-after commodity. In an effort to improve the quality of this resource, the Florida Department of Environmental Protection and the Environmental Protection Agency developed a program to analyze and collect data on the level of pollutants in Florida's waters. This program, the Watershed Management Basin Rotation Project, divides Florida's waters into 52 basins and places each of these basins into one of five groups. Each group undergoes a five-year assessment.

In the first phase, the FDEP analyzes data from the past 10 years to develop a list of waters within each basin that are potentially impaired by contaminants. Group 4, which includes the 2,100-square-mile Withlacoochee Basin and four others, entered this rotation in 2003. Of the 151 water body segments identified in the Withlacoochee Basin, 24 were listed as potentially impaired.

In the second phase, which is nearly complete for the Withlacoochee, the FDEP creates a list of verified impaired waters based on a detailed, 18-month analysis of data from the past seven-and-a-half-years. Confirmed impaired waters contain levels of certain pollutants higher than are permissible for the water to fulfill its designated purpose, such as for drinking or recreation.

These impaired waters then enter the final three phases

of the program, aimed to bring the contaminants in these waters to acceptable levels. The FDEP first develops a Total Maximum Daily Load (TMDL), a determination of the maximum amount of a given pollutant a water body can absorb and still maintain its designated uses. Once it adopts a TMDL, it develops and implements a plan of action to meet that TMDL. At the end of five years, the process restarts.

Florida's current system of water-quality assessment is a model for other states. Improving water quality, however, requires responsible management of land and water, says Tom Singleton, the FDEP's Withlacoochee River basin manager. He cites Homosassa Springs as an example, where a large volume of visitors has decreased water clarity and sea grass growth.

"We're kind of loving these resources to death," he says.

A suit brought by environmental group EarthJustice that challenged Florida's adherence to the Clean Water Act of 1977 resulted in the Florida Watershed Restoration Act of 1999. The act required an overhaul of the FDEP's management of the state's waters, part of which included a revamped method of assessing water quality. Thus, the basin rotation program began in 2000.

"The old solution to pollution is dilution," Singleton says. The rationale: When dispersed through enough water, a pollutant is too diffuse to cause a problem. This theory is valid, but only to a point; continue on this course, and eventually there will be too many contaminants present to offset their effects.

"We used to think that just because we couldn't detect something, it couldn't hurt us."

***

Captain Mike rises from his seat behind the steering

wheel, walks to the front of the boat and steps over the gate bearing "Best of the Best" stickers from the Citrus County Chronicle every year since 2000. He stoops out of sight for a moment, then stands, holding up a juice glass full of river water.

In the river, the water is a dark tea brown; a result of the tannic acid that dead leaves release into it. This darkness, however, is exacerbated by a layer of black muck nearly a foot deep in some places on the river bottom, Captain Mike explains. Fifty or sixty years ago, white sand covered 90 percent of the river bottom. But that was before the river had a problem with hydrilla, an invasive species. In order to stop it from clogging the river, the state uses herbicides to kill the hydrilla, which over several decades has formed muck on the river bottom.

But for some swirling particles and a slight pinkish brown tinge, the water in Captain Mike's glass is surprisingly clear.

"Oh," he adds, hoisting the glass a little higher. "Anybody want a drink?"

***

In the late 1990s, 45,000 fish died in a single fish kill in Lake Rousseau, a man-made lake not far from where Captain Mike leads today's tour. The culprit? In part, insufficient dissolved oxygen, the most frequent water-quality problem in the Withlacoochee River Basin. It is a factor in 14 of the 24 water bodies on the potentially impaired list.

But, Singleton notes, an oxygen deficit can occur naturally. In the slow moving, often shallow waters of the Withlacoochee, sunlight encourages growth of vegetation. These plants use oxygen that would otherwise be dissolved in the water.

Though the FDEP does investigate the causes of an

oxygen deficit, "we tell folks not to get too excited," Singleton says.

The second most common impairments in the Withlacoochee Basin; an overabundance of nutrients such as nitrogen in the water and mercury in fish, concern the FDEP more than low dissolved oxygen levels. Both are likely to result from human activity and threaten environmental and human health.

Excess nitrogen can cause aquatic vegetation to bloom excessively, choking waterways and killing fish. In drinking water, it can cause reproductive problems, as well as cancer and blood disorders in adults and children. In wildlife mercury can cause slower growth, abnormal behavior, decreased fertility and death. Human consumption of mercury-contaminated fish, which is the most common form of mercury exposure, can cause brain and nerve damage.

Historically, point-source pollution, such as industrial waste and sewage dumping, received the most attention. That type of water pollution is now basically under control, and now the major source of water pollution derives from ground runoff and the air, Singleton says. This type of pollution is more difficult to control, since everything from using fertilizers (which contain nitrogen) to waste burning (which releases mercury into the atmosphere) to cars braking (which leaves cadmium on the roadway) contributes to this diffuse-type of water pollution.

The Withlacoochee and other water bodies face a real threat from this non-point source pollution. Singleton recalls when he worked on water quality in South Florida and some fish developed ulcers, multiple sets of scales and fins and other abnormalities. They determined cadmium and zinc were the principal culprits.

Two portions of the lower Withlacoochee River, where

Captain Mike leads today's trip, have been verified as impaired for dissolved oxygen and mercury. Compared to others around the state, the basin as a whole has a relatively low number of impairments. Development has not yet encroached on the Withlacoochee as much as it has in other parts of the state, Singleton says; in many places, the river remains largely unchanged from 100 years ago.

"[The Withlacoochee] gives one a sense of how things used to be," he says. It helps people "understand how far other places need to go to improve water quality."

***

The older women on Captain Mike's boat shudder when he tells them that March is the ideal month to see snakes on the Withlacoochee. Fresh from hibernation, often they lay unmoving on the river banks.

"We do have a lot of snakes," he says. Forty-four species in Florida, to be exact. He chuckles. "Only 44!"

Just five of them are poisonous: the diamondback, pigmy and timber rattlesnakes, the coral snake and ("the most dangerous snake of all") the water moccasin. Moccasins will not only chase people and bite them in the water, Captain Mike says, but "they've also been known to climb into boats and bite people."

His comment hangs for a moment.

"So we stay out of those areas," Captain Mike continues. "People tend not to come back when them things happen."

Around a few more bends in the river, a cypress tree extends through a deck built over the river. It is massive not in height but girth, and its weathered gray bark contrasts the feathery spring green of its needles. These trees grow about one inch in diameter in 40 years, Captain Mike says. One like this could be from 1,000 to 1,500 years old.

These trees are Civil War veterans. They have seen floods, freezes, and hurricanes; have stood quietly for centuries as the river and its ever-changing traffic flows past: alligators, river otters, Indians, pontoon boats, and, more recently, airboats.

***

Sitting inside his home along the Withlacoochee, Ron Johnson can't carry on a conversation when the louder airboats pass by. In his five years living there, Johnson estimates there has been a 30 percent increase in the amount of airboat traffic on the river.

As a spokesman for a group of several hundred trying to make the airboats quieter, Johnson has pitted himself against a well-organized airboat lobby.

After three years of County Commission meetings, petitions, and working with state representatives, senators and even the governor, a measure went before the Citrus County Commission on April 12 to require airboat noise be no more than 90 decibels at 50 feet. Ninety decibels is about the amount emitted by a garbage disposal or an electric drill; extended exposure to noise over 85 decibels causes hearing damage. Similar legislation recently passed in neighboring Marion County.

"It's grassroots politics. You've just got to keeping hammering after it," Johnson says. For him, the need to quiet the airboats is obvious.

"If you lived on the river, you'd know the answer to that."

But airboaters argue that the "90 at 50" limit isn't practical.

"Have you ever made a margarita?" asks Bob Hoover Jr., president of the Citrus County Airboat Alliance. "Well, your blender just did 95 decibels!"

Hoover's organization favors making mufflers mandatory, which would help the noise problem, he says. Once a boat reaches a certain RPM, however, the propellers produce the majority of the noise. Quieter propellers cost more.

"I don't know where 90 came up. It seems like that's the magic number," Hoover says. "And it's not feasible."

The County Commission agreed. The measure failed, three votes to one.

***

The first alligator, no longer than a person's arm, clings to a small branch just above the surface of the water. The sun glints off its reptilian eye. Motionlessly, it watches as Captain Mike guides the boat slowly past.

A few feet away, two more come into view. Captain Mike's gators have not let him down. Each gator is slightly larger than the one before it. The mid-March sun seeps into their leathery hide, and not a blink betrays their stillness.

"Are you sure they're real? They're here all the time?" asks one passenger, a well-manicured woman of about 65.

"I'll be glad to let you off any time you want," Captain Mike responds. The woman laughs and declines the invitation. He explains that although people want to see the gators move, he doesn't like to disturb them.

Just past the gators, the boat nears a dead end. Captain Mike executes a three-point turn and retraces his path. But for a faint vibration of the seats, there's no indication that the four-cycle Yamaha motor is even running. The boat eases past the gators once more, closer this time. Eva and Skip, two visitors from Kentucky, scramble for their disposable camera.

A whirring noise filters through the cypress trees, distant at first then growing more insistent.

"Here come the airboats," Captain Mike says.

Within a minute, what sounds like a giant fan turned on high has drowned out the bird calls emanating from the tree canopy. Captain Mike and his passengers watch as its source appears from around a bend in the river.

An unsmiling man of about 60, wearing sunglasses and black ear muffs, sits in the driver's seat of the purple-glitter striped airboat. He slows when he sees Captain Mike's tour, and a throaty "chug-chug-chug" replaces the whirring. Captain Mike's boat bobs in the wake.

With a splash, the second gator falls from its perch. It struggles to regain its balance, reaching with one scaly arm and then another to climb back on the log. Its hide glistens after the dip in the 63-degree water.

The airboat picks up speed and disappears downriver. For a moment Captain Mike and his passengers are silent. High in the trees, the birds resume their song.

"It's amazing the birds are still chirping," Captain Mike says. His tone turns to disgust. "We're just losing so much along our waterways from just normal stuff, without having to do crap like this."

stream cleaning

Mike Burden, University of Missouri

A pool table, two prosthetic limbs, three propane tanks, 11 refrigerators, 173 tires, a keg, a toilet, two messages in bottles and three televisions. Items in a scavenger hunt? No. This is a small sample of what Missouri River Relief hauled out of the Missouri River in one day on one of its major river cleanups.

The trash in Missouri's waterways is an eyesore and causes wildlife habitat destruction, while toxic materials such as cigarette butts threaten aquatic life. But discarded kitchen appliances and couches aren't the only form of pollution drifting down Missouri's waterways. Every day, hundreds of millions of gallons of wastewater from sewage treatment plants flow into the Missouri and Mississippi rivers and Missouri streams without being disinfected for bacteria. Chemicals and metals from lawn care, farming, industry and mining also end up in Missouri's water and can endanger aquatic life and human health.

But the pressing financial issue facing the state now will be disinfecting wastewater to make waterways safe for swimming. The Missouri Department of Natural Resources has developed new standards for Missouri's waterways to bring the state closer to the 1972 Clean Water Act goal of making all waterways fishable and swimmable. The standards are on their way to the state attorney general's office and must be approved by the Environmental Protection Agency by April 2006, or the EPA will set the standards for the state.

The standards will hold 22,000 miles of Missouri waterways, including the Missouri and Mississippi rivers and 14 streams in Columbia, to a swimmable standard. This means that the water entering natural streams must have less than 200 colonies of fecal coliform, the bacteria in human and animal waste, and less than 126 colonies of E. coli per hundred milliliters of water. Currently, approximately 5,000 miles meet this swimmable standard. Also, the settlement calls for any wastewater facility within two miles of a classified waterway, or one that flows year-round, to disinfect the water leaving its plant.

The impetus for the upgrades was a December settlement between the EPA and the Missouri Coalition for the Environment. Ted Heisel, president of the coalition, says it was tired of the state dragging its feet on complying with the Clean Water Act.

Trent Stober, president of Columbia-based MEC Water Resources, says the cost for the regulated community to meet the new standards could be in the billions. "People are going to have to pay higher sewer rates, and I am concerned about that," he says.

In Boone County, 35 million gallons of wastewater flow into Perche Creek, Grindstone Creek, Hinkson Creek and other waterways. Only 13 of 126 wastewater facilities in the county are monitoring their effluent for fecal coliform. In the entire state, only a third of the nearly 3,000 facilities do the same.

Tom Ratermann, general manager at Boone County Regional Sewer District, says the district will have to invest $300,000 to upgrade 43 of its facilities to comply with the new standards. The estimate is based on the money needed to purchase the equipment and doesn't account for operating costs. The district's annual operating budget is $1.5 million. "Rate payers pay for those changes," Ratermann says. "Is that the best bang for your environmental buck? Are we prepared to spend the money for the 12 people who swim in Hinkson Creek?"

Whether they are huge facilities pumping hundreds of millions of gallons of wastewater into the Mississippi

River, such as the Metropolitan Sewer District of St. Louis, or small wastewater lagoons such as the one at Green Hills Mobile Home Park in Columbia, all facilities have the same three options. They can demonstrate that they already meet the standard. They can prove people aren't swimming in their local waterway, and therefore they won't have to disinfect. Or they can disinfect their wastewater to bring bacteria levels to the swimmable standard using chlorine or ultraviolet radiation.

The Green Hills Mobile Home Park pumps its wastewater into Perche Creek after passing it through a lagoon. Fred Burks, the owner, says he was informed of the new standards.

"Right now we're not exactly sure how we fall into it," Burks says. "If I have to go to a chemical type of treatment, I've had estimates of $30,000 to $50,000 just to have the system put in." He says he'll have to pass the additional costs on to his renters.

Behind the curve

Are Missourians ready to pay for cleaner water?

Some visitors to the Grindstone Nature Area agreed that the standards are needed, and most are willing to pay additional money to achieve them.

"I think it would be worth it," Justin Dijak, a cook, says. "My first instinct is 'finally [government is] spending money on something productive.' Especially on the conditions of the streams I've seen."

"If Missouri had adopted better standards sooner, we wouldn't have to play catch up now," Courtney Kerns, a natural biologist, says. "As to the cost to me, I would prefer that more of my taxes go to the environment."

But some people in the business of wastewater are worried about that cost. "I cannot meet these standards today," says Mary West, the director of Moberly Public Utilities.

Although many municipal operators are concerned about the cost, environmentalists point to the fact that this law has been in place for more than 30 years, and states were supposed to comply by 1983. "I don't know why Missouri was allowed to ignore federal law for the past 21 years," says Ken Midkiff of the Sierra Club.

Thirty-one states, including Missouri neighbors Kansas and Illinois, have established the fishable and swimmable standard. Sharon Watson, communications director for the Kansas Department of Health and Environment, says the financial impact on Kansas businesses has been minimal. This is because for the past decade, KDHE has taken a proactive approach and required facilities discharging into their streams to increase the amount of disinfection in their system or make other upgrades to reduce the bacteria.

So why is Missouri behind the curve? Recreation on the water generates millions of dollars each year, and Missouri has some of the most pristine national waterways, including the Eleven Point, Jack's Fork and Current rivers.

Thousands of volunteers across the state are removing the trash dumped in the rivers and streams, but the Missouri Department of Natural Resources, the agency charged with protecting Missouri's natural resources, has only a handful of people conducting chemical tests across the state's water bodies.

John Ford is one of them. He has spent the past 28 years wading in Missouri's waterways, cooling off after watching birds from the banks of a stream in his spare time and collecting samples for the Department of Natural Resources. In his sojourns through the water, Ford has twice contracted illnesses from bacteria. He samples streams near wastewater discharge plants to detect if the effluent flowing out of their pipes is depleting oxygen from the water and threatening sunfish, bass, frogs or any of the other critters that call the waterways home. For data on bacteria harmful to humans such as fecal coliform and E. coli, MDNR relies on the United States Geological Survey's 66 water quality monitoring stations around the state.

"To do a good job we would need about 28 staff," says Scott Totten, the soil and water protection division director with MDNR. "We have eight."

Missouri does have a State Revolving Fund that is used to help cities pay for environmentally friendly upgrades. But through the next year, President George W. Bush plans to cut the national budget for this program from $1.1 billion to $750 million. This means that federal backing for Missouri's fund will decrease from $30 million to $19 million. This leaves MDNR more dependent on the fees they receive from granting business permits.

"When budgets get cut, we have to get permits out the door, and that is more important than monitoring," Totten says. Between 60 and 70 percent of MDNR's water pollution program and 100 percent of its storm water management program are paid for by permit fees.

Getting the trash out takes time, energy and cultural change, but reducing the bacteria requires cash and information. MDNR estimates that 911 facilities around the state will need more than $300 million to upgrade their facilities to make more waterways swimmable.

Beyond the storm drain

For paddlers such as Joel McCune, water quality issues are a daily concern. He grew up paddling on the Big Piney and Buffalo rivers in northern Arkansas.

"My first memories are on the water," McCune says.

When he is not working on his master's degree in parks, recreation and tourism at MU, he is paddling his canoe in Finger Lakes, Gans Creek or other local waterways to train for the upcoming U.S. team trials in white-water slalom. McCune says sewage treatment is improving but not at the rate that it needs to, and the biggest problem is addressing nonpoint source pollution – pollution from multiple sources, such as agricultural and urban runoff.

"As long as we can turn on the lights, flush the stool and turn on the faucet and get water, we don't really care," says Bob Broz, a water quality specialist at MU Agricultural Extension. Broz says the community needs more watershed stewardship. "How do my actions affect someone else or the environment is the big question we need to ask," he says.

Last year, Representative Dennis Wood (R-Kimberling City) sponsored statewide legislation to provide an opportunity for unincorporated areas to do just that. His bill would allow areas such as Harg outside Columbia to access the state's revolving fund for wastewater upgrades.

"Water knows no boundaries," Wood says. "What's under your property today is under mine tomorrow, and you have no right to pollute it. We can't afford not to protect our water."

Volunteers and clean-water advocates across the state and especially around Columbia, which boasts the highest concentration of stream teams in the state, are taking action to achieve these goals. They are directing their efforts at the nonpoint source pollution. The EPA reports that storm water runoff is "one of the most significant sources of contamination in our nation's waters." This is especially the case in waterways such as Hinkson Creek, the backbone of Columbia's streams.

Where does the pollution come from?

Rain washes off the sidewalks, through the parking lots and down the streets and carries with it antifreeze, lawn chemicals, tons of trash and anything else that lies on the thousands of acres of impervious surface around town.

"Rampant residential development is a big problem,"

says Scott Hamilton, an urban conservationist with Show-Me Clean Streams. "We need to enforce stricter standards on developers clearing the ground. People need to realize that the storm drain right by their house flows directly into the streams."

Most of the water drains directly into Hinkson Creek, which meanders 11 miles through Columbia, collects 60 percent of the raindrops that fall on Columbia and is currently listed as an impaired waterway due to this nonpoint source pollution.

"What's going on in Hinkson Creek is going on in every city in Missouri that size and all over the country," said Leanna Zweig, a fish kill and pollution investigator for the Department of Conservation. "We're all downstream from someone else."

That is the message that Mona Menezes, the storm water outreach coordinator for Columbia, is trying to spread. After growing up on the Niangua River, Menezes now works to educate citizens by organizing stream clean ups, holding lawn-care seminars and other efforts. She says many Columbians believe storm water is treated at the wastewater treatment plant and that a watershed is a type of building.

In her own neighborhood, Menezes received a report on a woman picking up her dog's waste in a plastic bag and dumping it into the storm drain. Recently, she contacted a man who poured leftover wood stain in the drain and explained to him that the water ends up in Rock Bridge State Park.

"Every cigarette butt, plastic bag and other trash that isn't properly disposed of ends up in our city's streams," Menezes says. Fifty percent of the trash she has collected in streams has been plastic bags such as the ones used at Wal-Mart.

Menezes has led the charge to place the blue decals

that read "No Dumping/Drains to Stream" on the storm water drains around Columbia. Her volunteers have placed more than 400 of the decals around the city, and she says eventually they hope to have one on every drain.

She leads stream cleanups around Columbia at least twice a month during the warmer months. In March, she gathered the Fun City youth group at Flat Branch Creek. When the kids weren't distracted by tossing rocks or looking for frogs, they filled 32 red mesh bags with plastic Bud Light cups, Twix wrappers and other trash.

Menezes is also coordinating a healthy lawns program with Hamilton. Their program will be city-wide this summer. According to EPA reports, pesticides from lawns create three times more chemical waste in waterways than agricultural production. Together, Hamilton and Menezes are trying to educate the community about how to have a beautiful and watershed-friendly lawn.

Hamilton will host a rain garden workshop April 9, and he says there are already a dozen people who want to install the gardens this spring. Rain gardens use native wetland plants such as cattails to absorb and treat rainwater in yards. "Somebody could install one in one weekend," Hamilton says.

He also invited Jeff Zimmerschied to speak to people interested in watershed-friendly lawn care earlier this month. Zimmerschied is a former Monsanto employee who has transformed his career from convincing people chemicals are good to demonstrating how to care for land without them. He now owns a natural lawn-care company. "It isn't what you know but what you are willing to learn," he says. "People have been trained by TV to spray, spray, spray, and most homeowners don't take the time to read the label."

Below the surface

Farmers in Boone County are taking action, too. Ken Struemph administers the Special Area Land Treatment Program in Boone County. The aim of SALT is to improve water quality through farming practices. Struemph says in the past three years farmers have added 400 feet of stream bank stabilization, modified 1,300 acres of pasture, installed eight ponds and more in an effort to improve soil and water quality in the upper Hinkson watershed. Farmers can get 75 percent of the cost covered through the program, which has an annual budget of $464,000. Much of the funding comes from the one-tenth of one percent sales tax in Missouri that goes to parks and soil conservation.

For private landowners, there is the Environmental Quality Incentive Program through the Natural Resources Conservation Service. It is designed to fund projects that preserve wildlife habitat and reduce nonpoint source pollution, emissions, soil erosion and sedimentation. Taken together the practices can improve water and soil quality.

So what's the best way to look at water quality now? Until Missouri comes into compliance with the new standards, there are visual cues to look for to help determine whether a particular stream is a good place to splash around in.

"A lot of people call me and ask if it is safe to swim, and basically I tell them if the water is turbid and muddy, that's a bad time to go swimming because that means there is a lot of surface runoff, and bacteria is coming in," Ford says.

Hamilton looks at the critters living in the stream to determine its health. A few weeks ago he found only mosquito larvae and worms living in Flat Branch Creek – indicators of unhealthy water. Crayfish, mussels, mayfly larvae and stonefly larvae are usually good signs that the stream is fairly healthy. Hamilton says to monitor by checking bugs because they reveal the presence of pollution.

Although Missouri's water isn't always clear, one thing is: improving it will require cultural change and lots of cash, and the effort will affect everyone from environmentalists to industry leaders, farmers to factory workers, and paddlers to homeowners.

Here's how to start protecting Missouri's waters in your own backyard:

1) Plant native plants such as bluestem, which do not require synthetic fertilizers or pesticides.

2) Install a rain garden to collect and naturally filter runoff from your yard.

3) Mow properly. Zimmerschied suggests mowing on the tallest setting when grass is 3.5 to 4 inches long. Leave the clippings behind to provide nutrients to the grass and soil.

4) Clean up pet waste and garbage. When it rains, these pollutants wash into storm sewers that drain directly to local streams.

5) Join a stream team to help clean up trash, and learn how to conduct basic water quality tests.

6) If you choose to use chemicals in your yard, consult an expert and use them sparingly.

7) Work to preserve wooded buffer zones around streams that provide shade and absorb nutrients and sediment from surface runoff.

8) Take your car to the car wash, where water is reused several times before they send it to the sewer system for treatment.

First Printed in the Columbia Missourian

over medicated

Brad Parker, University of Missouri

Sara's* drug use began in the sixth grade. She was fidgety at school, so her doctor diagnosed her with Attention Deficit Disorder (ADD) and prescribed Ritalin. She used the drug until she was a sophomore in high school. During her sophomore year, she spent three or four months supplementing her prescribed dosage with another three or so pills at night to help her study before voluntarily giving up the medication altogether.

"I got great grades," Sara says. "But I'd stay up for three or four days straight. When I stopped taking it for two or three days, I'd crash."

During her senior year of high school, Sara's doctor prescribed a different medication for her. Sara does not know why there was a switch, but her doctor began prescribing Concerta – an encapsulated, time-release drug designed to circumvent the Ritalin abuse that had become prevalent nationwide in the previous year or two. Still, Sara and her friends discovered how to cut open the capsules, scoop out the medication and snort it like cocaine to get a buzz.

Sara had a prescription for Concerta until her sophomore year at MU. She was supposed to take one or two pills per day, depending on how much studying she had to do. Instead, she irregularly took pills to help her focus and saved the others to crush and snort for fun on the weekends.

Snorting the stimulants allows them to enter the bloodstream more rapidly and in a greater concentration through the nasal membranes. It also magnifies the common side effects, including headaches, jitters, tics, moodiness, insomnia, stomachaches and loss of appetite.

After Sara gave up her Concerta prescription because she felt that she didn't need it anymore, she would use her friends' medications, including Adderall. It is a more powerful medication that provides a stronger buzz when abused. When those highs were not enough, she and her friends started using cocaine.

Sara's slide into drug abuse characterizes a growing concern about college students illegally using Attention-Deficit/Hyperactivity Disorder (AD/HD) medications – including Ritalin, Concerta, Adderall, Dexedrine and Metadate – as a study aid or party drug.

Variably referred to as ADD, ADHD and AD/HD over the years, the diagnosis Attention-Deficit/Hyperactivity is now contained in the American Psychiatric Association's Diagnostic and Statistic Manual, Fourth Edition, an evidence-based listing of mental disorders. This reflects the different forms the condition can take. As an umbrella term, AD/HD can describe individuals who either exhibit symptoms of inattention, hyperactivity or impulsivity, or both.

A study published in the January/February issue of the Journal of American College Health reports AD/HD drug abuse might be approaching the prevalence of cocaine and marijuana use. On the campus where the researchers conducted their study, 17 percent of the 179 surveyed men and 11 percent of the 202 surveyed women abused prescription stimulants. Nearly half of the surveyed students – 44 percent – said they knew others who used stimulants for academic or recreational reasons.

People sometimes refer to AD/HD medications as "academic steroids" or "smart drugs" because they improve concentration. By increasing levels of the neural transmitter dopamine in the brain, the medications help people with the disorder combat the restlessness and inattention that often results in unfinished assignments, daydreaming and sloppy work. In small doses, they give people with normal dopamine levels an almost superhuman ability to concentrate.

Academic performance seems to be a secondary motivation for abuse, says Dr. Paul Robinson, associate clinical professor of child health and director of adolescent medicine at MU. "I think the primary motivation is recreational," he says, based on interviews with his patients. "I think it's to get a high."

Sara says she does not know anyone in college who actually needs AD/HD medication. "I'll be honest," she says. "I didn't need it. I grew out of my ADD like most people do. It was more recreational than academic – maybe even all recreational."

Many college students heavily abuse Adderall because it provides the strongest, longest high and the fewest unwanted side effects, Sara says. "It's extremely prevalent," she adds. "I know people who use Adderall more than anything else."

Elizabeth Burns, program director for Boonville Valley Hope, says prescription drug abuse in general is increasing in the area. She says many current and former MU students seek rehabilitation at Valley Hope, a 65-bed treatment center for people with chemical dependencies. Painkillers are the most commonly abused prescription drugs among college-age people, she says, with ADD medications next on the list.

Robinson says students often try to work the system to get unnecessary prescriptions. "Kids are coming in and acting like they have ADD so they can get high on the medication or give it to their friends."

Doctors are on the lookout for those pretenders,

however. And physicians and psychologists should work together to prevent misdiagnosis, Robinson says. Some learning disabilities and health problems, such as lead poisoning and sleep disorders, have symptoms similar to AD/HD. Therefore, diagnoses should follow a thorough review of a patient's history in addition to psychological and medical testing.

"Too many people make the diagnosis without all of the proper information," Robinson says.

Because of the changing attitudes in American culture toward mental health, there has been a jump in diagnosis for mental health-related problems, Burns says. She also cites an increase in advertising among pharmaceutical sales companies as a reason that people are going to their doctors and demanding specific drugs.

"The problems lie with the individuals who have the propensity to have addictive personalities," Burns says. "That biological predisposition coupled with mood-altering medication creates a more likely scenario for drug abuse."

Burns offers the example of students who take illegal drugs, such as cocaine, then complain of mood swings and trouble concentrating. Doctors diagnose them with AD/HD and prescribe stimulants without realizing they actually are compounding a problem, she says.

Sara acknowledges there are legitimate uses for the medications. "You need Adderall and Ritalin for the people who really need it, but there will always be people around to abuse it," she says. "People are going to abuse drugs no matter what."

Taking a small dose of the medication – half a pill – helps focus, Sara says. In recreational settings, however, people take larger dosages to over-energize their bodies for a day or two.

"When you need it, you become centered," Sara says. "When you don't need it, you become unbalanced, energetic and hyper."

Sara says taking too much of her medication does not lower inhibitions or cloud memory. "It's like living in fast-forward, but you're fully aware of everything that's going on.

"You want to go to sleep, but there's nothing you can do to get to sleep. Once you do get to sleep, it's for really short periods until the drug gets out of your system."

Some AD/HD patients abuse their prescriptions. The typical result of abuse in those who are diagnosed with disorder, and in need of medication, is sleepiness – not the usually desired effect. It is more common, however, for them to give away or sell their pills and risk the consequences of not treating the disorder (if they actually have it), says Dr. Robinson.

Sara agrees. "A lot of students get a prescription so they can sell it," she says, adding that Adderall fetches about $5 per pill among students. In a pharmacy, the price is about $3 per pill.

Both ends of the transaction are illegal. Methylphenidate (Ritalin, Concerta or Metadate) and amphetamine (Adderall or Dexedrine) are controlled substances that present a high potential for abuse. Possessing those drugs without a prescription is a Class C felony, which carries up to a seven-year jail sentence. Unauthorized sale and distribution are Class B felonies, which can earn five to 15 years in jail.

Robinson says the risks associated with taking larger dosages of AD/HD medication seem minimal, and those who actually have the disorder are more tolerant of the drugs than recreational users are.

Robinson does not know the long-term consequences

of abusing AD/HD drugs. "My thought is that it would be the same as that of any stimulant: weight loss, depression when coming down from the drug, cardiac arrhythmias and other similar things," he says.

"One of the problems is that drug abuse in this population is almost never a 'pure' event," he says, speaking of the adolescents and young adults he has interviewed in his office. "Most who abuse stimulant drugs also abuse many other substances, including – perhaps – marijuana, tobacco and cocaine, which are equally dangerous."

Sara knows firsthand that problem behaviors tend to group. "People who use ADD medication recreationally use other stimulants along with it," she says. "And people who use another stimulant like cocaine replace it with Adderall when they can't get it because it's a similar high.

"If you want a better high, you go to the narcotics. You can meet people who will lead you into that other stuff, but you need to have strength to say no to it."

Although the AD/HD medications are not addictive for those who take them according to their prescriptions, the greater dosages achieved through snorting increase the likelihood for psychological dependency in abusers, Robinson says.

People who find themselves addicted to prescription medications can start on the road to recovery by being honest about their drug usage, Burns says. Then she advises a medical checkup because of the drugs' physical effects. Joining a support group and exploring outpatient or residential treatment are the next steps.

Addiction to prescription drugs is something that needs to be taken seriously and treated, she says. "It requires a lifestyle change."

Sara says everyone around a recreational prescription-drug abuser suspects or recognizes the problem. "Once you come clean with your friends, if they're real friends, they'll help you quit."

To head off abuse and addiction, there are controls on prescriptions, Robinson says.

Prescriptions for AD/HD medications cannot be written for refills, meaning patients must request new prescriptions from their doctors every time. If patients request a new, 30-pill prescription in fewer than 30 days, doctors will begin to ask questions about misuse.

Burns says it is also important for past or recovered abusers to notify their doctors about their previous prescription drug abuse.

"There is often an unaddictive alternative available, but doctors have to know that normal drug treatment could be problematic," says Burns.

Now a senior in MU's College of Arts and Science, Sara has not used drugs – prescription or otherwise – for approximately four months, and she is confident that she will stay clean. She says the one or two positives are not worth the huge number of negatives.

"No more for me. I'm done," she says. "My body is tired, and I've grown up. I'm not trying to rebel anymore."

Prescription drug abuse statistics

Attention-Deficit/Hyperactivity Disorder is a medical disorder that affects people of all ages. The most recognizable symptoms include distractibility, impulsivity and hyperactivity. The growing problem with AD/HD prescription drug abuse is explained in terms of the statistics below.

• 17% of 179 surveyed men and 11% of 202 surveyed women reported illicit use of prescribed stimulant medication.

• 44% of surveyed students said they knew students

who used stimulants for academic or recreational reasons.

• Students reported time pressures associated with college life and stated stimulants increased alertness and energy.

• According to the Drug Enforcement Administration, methylphenidate (Ritalin) production increased about 900% from 1990 to 2000, then 40% from 2000 to 2002 (introduction of Concerta and Metadate). Amphetamine (Dexedrine and Adderall) production increased 5,767% from 1993 to 2001.

• Recreational stimulant use is more frequent among 18- to 25-year-olds than any other age group.

• Babcock and Byrne (2000) found 16% of students at a Massachusetts public liberal arts college had tried methylphenidate recreationally, and 31% thought Ritalin was abused on campus.

• 3% of surveyed students had been or were diagnosed with AD/HD. About 3% had a prescription for AD/HD medication.

• 40% of students who had prescriptions had used them illicitly.

• Of abusers, 37% of the men and 29.2% of the women knew students who would provide them with stimulants.

• 22.3% of surveyed students said stimulants were used illicitly on campus.

• Insufficient sleep, combined with academic and social pressures, might lead college students to seek energy boosters and study aids.

• Illicit use of stimulants already might be approaching that of cocaine and marijuana.

Additional Percentages from the study:

63% preferred to take stimulants orally.

27% took stimulants during finals week.

21% took stimulants with other drugs.

15% took stimulants before tests.

15% took stimulants with alcohol.

14% thought stimulants helped their academics long-term.

12% took stimulants when they partied.

12% preferred to snort stimulants.

First Printed in the Columbia Missourian

Consumer Magazine Article: Service & Information

look familiar?

Erin Rietz, Ball State University

Every girl needs a fairy godmother. In the classic fairy tale, Cinderella needed the enchanting assistance of a helpful little lady to create the beautiful gown that would bring out her inner princess as she attended the ball of her dreams.

Although Angie Abrams-Rains may not possess such magical powers, this bubbly Ball State journalism instructor serves as the fairy godmother to high school girls across east central Indiana through her passionate devotion to an organization she founded less than a year ago. '

When teenage girls find the demands of the high school prom to be too much, they can turn to Abrams-Rains' project, the Great Gown Giveaway, for help.

Last spring, Abrams-Rains perused a Web site for The Princess Project, an organization based in San Francisco that collects and distributes used prom dresses to area high school students. Soon after, she began to get ideas.

The Princess Project has helped more than 2,000 girls in the last two years, and Abrams-Rains wanted to help. She and graduate assistant Amie Morehead considered sending some of their old formal dresses to the charity, but instead they decided that the project was such a good idea that they would start their own version in Muncie.

GOWN GATHERERS UNITE

Little did they know how quickly the Great Gown Giveaway would grow. Abrams-Rains and Morehead enlisted the help of two other women from the Department of Journalism. Christi Girton, another staff member, and Jennifer Woods, a journalism undergraduate student, joined the effort, and the group members almost immediately began having meetings to establish the role of the organization.

The Great Gown Giveaway would seek to provide girls with all of the components they need for the prom, the women decided. They planned to open the service to all east central Indiana high school students, but the women mainly focused on Delaware County from the beginning.

Abrams-Rains smiles widely with an excited twinkle in her eyes as she talks about every aspect of the Great Gown Giveaway. "I just think that every girl deserves to go to prom," Abrams-Rains says. "I think every girl should have that one night to feel great about herself."

Girton and Woods both attest to Abrams-Rains' fervor for the project and say that it is her enthusiasm that drives the group's success. They hope to eventually expand to the surrounding counties, particularly Jay and Randolph. Girls interested in obtaining a dress from the organization are not required to produce proof of financial need – all Great Gown Giveaway requires is to see a student ID, and the dress each girl chooses is hers to keep.

"You could be the wealthiest person in the town, but as long as you think you need a dress, that's all that matters," Abrams-Rains says.

FREE PRESS, 50 DRESSES

The original plan was to begin collecting dresses in time to donate them in the spring of 2005. However, a reporter from the Star Press learned about the project last spring and wrote a story about it that the ladies say gave them a head start. "It just kind of blossomed all at once from that," Abrams-Rains says. "We got about 50 calls just that first day from people who wanted to give us dresses."

Following the publication of the article, the Great Gown Giveaway prom dress collection began to form. Mainly because of the free publicity, the ladies say they were able to help girls from five area high schools obtain free dresses for their proms.

"It was just amazing that even through a small story in the newspaper so many people would pick up on it," Girton says. "With our lack of promotion at that point, it was great to have so many people get wind of it."

Following such a quick and successful start, the women were excited to make big plans for their second year. Although Abrams-Rains says Morehead left the group due to time constraints, the three remaining members began to set goals for a Spring Extravaganza that would be held before the 2005 prom season.

"Basically at the extravaganza the girls can just show up with a school ID and we can fit them all with the whole works," Abrams-Rains says.

NOT YET NONPROFIT

The group hopes the extravaganza will include not only dresses, but also everything else that makes up the traditional prom ensemble such as accessories, shoes and even hair and make-up tips from area businesses. "It's kind of like a bridal show for prom stuff," Girton says.

Despite all of the early success and plans, however, things have not been trouble-free for the women of the Great Gown Giveaway. Girton says they held a callout for dresses and accessories earlier in the fall but only collected a few dresses. Also, sudden illness within the organization has slowed down the group's progress and brought some initiatives to a temporary halt.

The women say one of the most frustrating problems

is lack of financial stability. Although they received some donations following the Star Press article, much of the money was used while filing for nonprofit status with the government – recognition the Great Gown Giveaway still has yet to receive.

Abrams-Rains says some would-be donors have committed to helping out, but not until the nonprofit status has been obtained.

Woods says the organization has had its problems this year, but everything will pick up soon enough. "Once we get that nonprofit status, I think things could start falling into place," Woods says. "It's really like a domino effect."

Abrams-Rains already has plans for the money once the organization receives it. She says the organization would like to have the ability to hold more fund-raisers and actually buy dresses in the odd sizes that are hard to come by. Also, Girton says she hopes to get more money so that the women can promote the organization more heavily.

The women of the Great Gown Giveaway plan to have a second callout sometime this spring semester, and they are looking for a variety of donations from the public.

DONORS, DON'T DISCRIMINATE

Abrams-Rains says people and businesses can donate any type of formal dress, shoes, accessories, gift certificates for hair and make-up appointments, or even just their time – volunteers will be needed to ensure that the Spring Extravaganza is a success.

The Great Gown Giveaway will not turn down any kind of donation. Girton says that although the women may not be able to give away dresses unsuitable for a modern-day prom, they would take them off anyone's hands.

Abrams-Rains, who currently keeps two large racks of dresses in her home's guest room until the organization can afford a storage facility, says she has some dresses that were probably worn in the '70s and '80s.

"We've got some horrible dresses," Abrams-Rains says. "But then again, we've got some gorgeous, some absolutely amazing dresses."

Although Girton insists that Abrams-Rains has spear-headed everything, her own excitement for the project is based on a feeling of satisfaction in helping others. "Just seeing how happy it made the few people we have helped already has made it all worthwhile," Girton says.

"We don't want them to think it's a hand-me-down or a gimme. We just want them all to have that special experience."

First Published in Expo Magazine

you can refuse booze!

Dana Schmidt, Iowa State University

Let's face it. If you haven't been offered alcohol by now, chances are you soon will. Deciding whether to drink is a big decision and when you've seen the most popular girl in your school or the cutest guy in your math class take a sip at a party; it's hard to resist the temptation. Here are some tips from teens that've been in your shoes to help you refuse alcohol.

Just Say "No." You've undoubtedly heard this phrase before, but in many situations it's all you need to do. Jessica H., 18, from Aberdeen, S.D., was 16 years old when she was first asked to drink alcohol. She had gone to a classmate's house after school just to hang out. "I didn't know the person very well and she ended up having alcohol there and asked me if I wanted some to drink," Jessica H. says. "I said no. A simple no was all it took for me."

Laura, 17, from Strafford, N.H., says she's also been pressured to drink. "It's a little intimidating when you have a peer asking you to do something you really don't want to do. It's nerve racking to say no, but after you've said no, people will usually leave you alone."

Be Confident. If someone senses you're hesitant in saying no, he or she might pressure you even more. "Everyone loves to take advantage of a weak person and boss him or her around," says Jawad, 18, from Owing Mills, Md. "If you don't cave into peer pressure, you will be a strong person and no one will be able to bring you down."

Also, if you're confident in saying no, the people pressuring you know you've already made the decision not to drink, so they might be less likely to keep pressuring you, Jessica H. says.

Give an Excuse. Okay. So saying no and being confident might not always work. If that happens you can give the person a reason why you don't want to drink. "Most people that I know are fine with someone not drinking, but if they keep insisting you could just say you're driving tonight or you're allergic to alcohol," says Kaleb, 17, from Red Bay, Ala.

Juli, 18, from Stowe, Vt., suggests you say, "My parents will kill me!" or "I hate beer. It tastes like piss." If you're in a sport at school, you can tell them "My coach will kill me!" or "I have a meet tomorrow so I can't," Jessica H. says.

Remember, you can always just tell the person you're not in the mood and ask for some soda instead, Jawad says. Even if you don't like soda, you can ask for something else to drink, such as water, milk, or juice.

But beware when someone offers punch or Kool-aid that has been sitting out on a table. Lots of times people will spike punch by adding some alcohol or even dangerous drugs to it. Never leave your soda can or glass of juice unattended because someone may try to put something in it. If you forget and leave your glass sitting around, just ask for a new alcohol-free drink.

Also, prepare a couple of excuses before you go to a party. That way you'll be ready if you're offered alcohol.

Leave the Situation. It's natural to feel alone and uncomfortable when it seems as if you're the only one not drinking at a party. Jessica B., 17, from Bloomington, Minn., says it's important you feel comfortable in every situation you're in. "My mom always tells me if you don't want to slip, don't put yourself in a slippery situation. If you don't feel safe at a party, than don't go."

If you do decide to go to a party and the people there

keep pressuring you and telling you that if you drink, "It'll be lots of fun," or "It'll loosen you up" or if they keep telling you how fun it will be for them to see you get drunk, find a way to leave the party. You can call your parents to come pick you up or have a friend who hasn't been drinking take you home.

"Your parents will understand if you call them and tell them you want leave the situation," Juli says. And she should know. When Juli was a freshman in high school she frequently carpooled to school with a girl from her town. One night before driving to a school event, Juli's friend suggested they go out to dinner. "When we got there her friends were sitting there smoking and drinking. I decided to leave and called one of my classmate's mothers. I didn't know the classmate very well, but her mom came and picked me up."

Find a Support System: It may seem as if you have to drink to be cool, but that's not true. You're a cool person – a way cooler person – if you choose not to drink because that means you can have fun without being intoxicated. Because you're such a cool person, there will be plenty of other cool people like you – people who choose not to consume alcohol – who you can hang out with. It's important to have friends and to surround yourself with people who share your same viewpoint about drinking. Having friends who don't drink is the best way to resist pressure because you can support each other and remind each other of your decision not to drink. "If you have friends who will only be your friends because you drink with them, than honestly you're too good for them," Laura says.

Juli knew a friend who felt as if she was the only one in her school who didn't drink, so Juli suggested she start a Students Against Destructive Decisions (SADD) chapter at her school. The girl, who attended a school of 150 students, had 10 people show up at the first meeting. "[The group] will help you be with people who have the same feelings as you do," Juli says.

It's tough to say no when you're pressured to drink alcohol – especially when it seems as if everyone else is doing it. But you can stay strong and resist the pressure if you really want to. And remember, someone who pressures you to do something you don't want to do really isn't a friend. Real friends accept you for who you are and respect your decisions.

Alcohol-Free Alternatives

The weekend is finally here and you've got nothing to do. Here are some ideas teens from the SADD National Leadership Council have for having alcohol-free fun:

Karaoke Night: Like singing and dancing? Then get some of your friends together and have a blast performing your favorite tunes for each other. To make things even more exciting, have your own American Idol contest where each week you vote off your friends until only one is left. Take the winner out to a movie or have all your friends chip in to get her a CD of her favorite group.

BYOB: No, no, no. BYOB does not stand for Bring Your Own Beer. It can stand for anything you want it to stand for, such as Bring Your Own Banana (to make banana splits, of course) or Bring Your Own Board game. Be creative and come up with your own fun BYOB night ideas.

Movie Marathon: Do you and your girlfriends think Chad Michael Murray is really cute? Then grab some popcorn, sodas, and your other favorite munchies and have a movie marathon night where you watch all the movies he's ever been in. Or, if you want to see lots of cute actors and not just Chad, have each of your friends choose her favorite movie and watch all of the movies in one night (or one weekend).

Play Dress Up: You're never too old to play dress up, so grab your friends and have some fun. Decide on a theme, dress up in funny outfits, and go out to dinner. You might get some weird looks from people, but you and your girlfriends will have a blast dressing silly for the evening.

Make a Difference: Spend your Saturday helping your community by volunteering at your local hospital, children's club, homeless shelter, or any other organization in your town. Lots of organizations everywhere need volunteers, gather your gal pals and choose a group! You will not only have fun –you'll be helping someone in need.

hoops and hollers

Basketball, Buffets, Booze and Bracket Busting
Adam Wright, Arizona State University

A Vegas son rises

It's 6:30 a.m. in Las Vegas, and Danny Bogen isn't sure whether his day is starting or ending.

He stretches, wipes the corner of his mouth and hits on a 12. The dealer turns over a face card and takes Danny's chips before his brain can even do the math.

Danny finally gets up from the blackjack table where he spent the night and decides to catch some winks.

On his way to the elevator he runs right into his father.

Most fathers would be disappointed to find their son just making it to bed at sunrise with an empty wallet after a night of craziness. But instead, Norm grabs Danny by the arm and steers him toward their home for the weekend: the sports book at the Golden Nugget.

Danny and Norm arrive at "the book" around 7 a.m. to find hundreds of fans wearing jerseys and hats, dragging coolers of beer and food, and holding piles of betting slips. Hundreds of potential dollars worth of paper slip into pockets and wallets as sports fans settle into seats in front of three huge TV screens. It's three full hours before the first game starts, yet March Madness has officially begun in the City of Sin.

Who needs the Super Bowl?

The first weekend of March Madness marks one of the biggest weekends of the year in Vegas. Starting March 17th with the first round, 64 college basketball teams battle their way toward the national championship. Fans can watch and bet on every single game. Some of those thousands of fans will leave town with a few "thousands" of their own.

Unlike the Super Bowl, where fans must wait to see who's playing before booking reservations, college basketball fans can expect at least one of their favorites to make the field every year. Jeremy Handel, public relations manager for the Imperial Palace, says the hotel starts receiving reservations for rooms during March Madness as early as fall of the previous year.

The Imperial Palace, or "the I.P." as it's affectionately known, devotes its bars, 230 individual TVs and 12 big screens to fans and gamblers. The bets and odds are listed on dry-erase boards behind the tellers.

The I.P. harkens back to the old days of Vegas; when the emphasis was on gambling rather than shopping and shows. The I.P. is loaded with card and dice games as well as countless slot machines and video poker. After the basketball games are over, the blackjack dealers become "Dealtainers" as they perform and deal cards dressed like Michael Jackson, Barbara Streisand and others.

Downtown, the Golden Nugget sets up a sports book in its main ballroom, which is enclosed by frosted windows, giving sports fans the feeling of being in a fishbowl looking out on the rest of the casino. Multiple big screen TVs as well as numerous smaller sets broadcast every game simultaneously.

Before each game, an announcer asks the crowd to cheer for the game they want on the main TV. The game that receives the loudest cheers is shown on the main TV, and the audio is pumped through the sound system.

The "Nugget" stations two tellers in the ballroom so bettors can place bets without leaving the room. Between games, hundreds of people often stand in line to place bets. Meanwhile cocktail waitresses cruise the room and serve drinks and delicacies, such as hot dogs and sandwiches, all weekend long.

The book at Caesar's Palace, one of the nicest and biggest in Vegas, has booths with individual TVs as well as big screens on the walls. Additional big screens list the bets, spreads and odds. The chairs are large and comfortable. The dark colors and cool lighting evoke a calm, luxurious mood.

Don't ever look away

It's 10 a.m.

The beers are flowing, and 4th-seed Maryland is about to tip off against 13th-seed UT-El Paso. The spread for the game is Maryland by 7 points.

Danny places his bet on UTEP because he likes betting against his dad and he knows just how much 7 points can be in the tournament. He also knows UTEP's shooting guard Chris Craig can shoot the lights out from anywhere, at any time.

The fans are fresh and rowdy for the first game, drinks are flowing and the announcer in the Golden Nugget sports book is keeping the crowd pumped up.

Maryland builds an 11-point lead with just 10 minutes to go in the game. The room starts to relax and Maryland bettors start thinking about cashing in their slips and hitting the nearest buffet.

Before anyone notices, UTEP rips off a 7-point run capped by a Chris Craig lay-up and Maryland's lead is cut to 4.

The spread is now in serious danger. The gamblers tense up. Palms get sweaty, knuckles turn white.

Some games are quite upsetting

Picking an upset is one of the best ways to make money because the odds are always longer. One place to look for upsets in the NCAA tournament is in the 12-5 game between the 12th-seeded team and the 5th-seeded team.

Since 1990, the 12th seed has upset the 5th seed 22 times, which translates to a 37 percent winning percentage. This upset has occurred at least once every year since 1990 except for the 2000 tournament.

Although a 16th seed is rarely as competitive as a 1st seed, by the 12-5 game the teams are much more evenly matched. The 5th seed is often overconfident and has a tendency to forget just how good the team they're facing in the first round might be.

In seven of the last 15 years, the 12th seed has beaten the 5th seed in two or more of the four games.

Money time

After Chris Craig buries a 3-pointer, the game is tied at 81 with 1:39 to go.

Danny and his brethren who picked the underdog start screaming. They know that if UTEP loses by no more than 6 points, they'll all still win big.

Bettors for the favorite start praying for overtime, because only in overtime can Maryland rebuild its 7-point lead and cover the spread.

UTEP fouls Maryland's D.J. Strawberry, who drains both free throws to put Maryland ahead 84-81 with just 47 seconds left.

Vegas is holding its breath.

There's still enough time for Maryland to extend the lead…or for UTEP to win.

UTEP scores.

84-83.

Maryland fans are just hoping to squeeze out a win at

this point. They'd be heartbroken if they lost their bets and their team in the same game.

Maryland makes two free throws.

86-83.

14 seconds left.

It's high noon. It's a showdown. Get the ball to the gunslinger, Chris Craig.

If UTEP misses Maryland advances and the spread is covered.

If they tie the game, Maryland bettors have a chance to beat the spread.

Maryland fans, Maryland bettors, UTEP fans and UTEP bettors, all in the same room, all with different hopes on the outcome, all with their butts on the utmost edge of their chairs.

The ball is in-bounded; Craig comes free, gets the ball and puts it up for the tie.

The shot is blocked.

Maryland fans exhale, but UTEP's Jason Williams picks up the ball with time left on the clock.

He passes back to Craig, who throws up a prayer at the buzzer, and it hits nothing but…

…nothing. It's an air ball. Fans cry for a foul, but none comes. The game finally ends.

Maryland wins by 3, but the spread is covered. Soon the floor of the room is also covered…with torn betting slips rendered meaningless by UTEP's inability to give up and go quietly.

But Danny and those who bet UTEP are winners of their first bet of the weekend.

That's how it goes in this town.

Beers pop open. Fans settle deeper into their seats,

take a deep breath and get ready for the second game. One down, 31 more to go.

A Bettor's Primer

Although betting in the sports book is a major step up from your yearly office pool, it's still one of the simplest bets in town. There are no cards to count, no little ball bouncing around on a circle of numbers, no cherries to line up, no bluffing – and you never need to wear sunglasses like the poker players on TV. It's simply feeling your hunch and placing your bet with a teller.

The first thing to know is the point spread or line, which is the number of points the favorite is expected to win by. It's also the number the experts know will compel half the bettors to bet for the favorite while enticing the other half to take a chance on the underdog. By betting on the favorite, you give the underdog the lead before the game starts because the favorite has to overcome this hypothetical lead for the bet to be a winner.

Here's an example. The New England Patriots were favored to win the 2005 Super Bowl by 6 points. The bet at the casino would look like this: Patriots –6/Eagles +6. Before the game even starts, you have to view the game as if the Eagles are already up by 6 points. The Patriots won by only 3, meaning that in Vegas, they lost by 3. The Patriots won the Super Bowl, but anyone who bet on them with the point spread lost the bet.

Another bet is the money line, which eliminates the point spread. Whoever wins the game, no matter if by one point or 100, wins the bet. This bet comes with odds. The lower the odds, the more it has a chance of happening.

The bet is written in the sports book like this: Suns +240/Spurs –280. This means the Spurs are favored. A

$100 bet on the Suns would win $240. You'd have to bet $280 on the Spurs to win $100.

Most casinos offer futures bets, which deal with games that are, well, in the future. For example: Let's say you bet $5 on the Washington Nationals (300:1) to win the 2005 World Series this coming October. If by some miracle they actually do, you'll win $1,500.

Betting the totals, also known as the over/under, doesn't require you to pick a winner. Instead, the casino sets a number of total points that two teams will score. You simply decide whether the teams' combined final score will add up to "over" or "under" the set score.

For example: The Suns beat the Jazz 136-128. The total was 264, definitely over the point total that any casino in the world would have set. If you'd bet the "over" on this game, you'd have been the big winner.

The parlay bet is one of the most exciting and lucrative bets in Vegas. Bettors pick two or more games, and if they all win, the winnings compound. The more games you pick, the higher the odds. A five-team basketball parlay at Bally's pays off at 20 to 1. If you bet $5 and win all five games, you get $100. Unfortunately, if just one team loses, you lose the whole bet.

Consumer Magazine Article: First Person

daddy's girl

Nicole Williams, Arizona State University

March 10, 2005 3:45 p.m.

Southwest Airlines Flight 251 from Phoenix to
Portland, Oregon isn't full. I have three seats all to myself.
Chunks of salad cling to the back seam of the middle seat
– a previous passenger's lunch. When I sit down I smell
Chinese food, and sure enough two rows back someone is
cramming down Panda Express.

The plane takes off. Soon we fly over the red bluffs
of the Colorado Plateau. The pilot says those of us seated
on the left side of the plane will be able to see the rim of
the Grand Canyon. The recycled air circulating inside the
plane makes my eyes sting.

It's my last spring break as an Arizona State University student. I'm going to graduate in a few months, and I
should be celebrating by traveling to Mazatlan or Cancun
or Rocky Point, the Mexican resorts that attract so many
ASU spring breakers. Instead, I'm going to visit Wayne
Williams, my father, a convicted child molester currently
incarcerated in Oregon.

I haven't seen Dad in nearly two years. I know I have
to go through with this planned visit, but it bothers me
that I am going to visit him at all. Why should I give
him the privilege of seeing me? It's like saying, "Hey, you
haven't been there for me in the past 21 years of my life,
but I'm going to visit you in prison."

Why do I feel this is a battle and I'm the one surren-
dering and he's the one winning? I want to turn the plane
back. It's going to be awkward tomorrow.

I'm going to ask my father if he molested my nine-
year-old stepsister.

I don't even want to know the truth. Yet again, I need to know the truth. Something inside me tells me that if I just ask him, he will deny he's a pedophile and it will all go away. So I will ask him and I will write a story about it for a journalism class. I have everything packed. I have my tape recorder, notebook and laptop; everything but the audio CD of his sentencing, which was sent to me a few weeks ago by the Deschutes County Circuit Court. I have not been able to bring myself to listen to it yet. I left the CD in Arizona

***

Nicola

…You were the one in my life that made life worth living when sometimes I wasn't doing very well. I will always remember and cherish these special times between you and I. These are the few little years that made you and me who we are as father and daughter, that I will always thank our heavenly father for…

Dad

***

My father is one of about 234,000 sex offenders in America, according to the Bureau of Justice Statistics. The bureau says one in four children fall victim to inappropriate touching by a sex offender. Eighty-five percent of the predators are known to the victim.

In November, 1994, 10 years before my father was sent to prison, Oregon voters approved Measure 11 in the Oregon State Legislature. The measure boosted mandatory minimum sentences for serious sex crimes. In 2004, Dad was sentenced under Measure 11 to six years in prison with no chance of parole for sexually abusing my stepsister. For the past six months, he has been serving his 75-month prison sentence in Two Rivers Correctional Facility in northeastern Oregon, in the isolated town of Umatilla, which is just across the Columbia River from Washington.

***

Nicola

...I'm finding that I have so many things I want to say and talk to you about, but I seem to get lost in all my thoughts and feelings. I pray that you and I still have time to spend together in this life. We've got a lot of catching up to do... so much unfinished business. So many things too, that we never had the opportunity to discuss, so we might have a better understanding of each other's feelings. You and I have been robbed of times that can never be caught or relived again, but I am thankful that not all has been lost...

Dad

***

I was the first person in the family he wrote from prison. When I received that first letter in August, 2004, I felt as if it was the only time he'd ever tried to show me he cared about me. And yet he spelled my name wrong. Nicola instead of Nicole.

***

I don't have very many memories of my dad. I remember times we went fishing. Rubber boots, hair in a pony tail, Levi jeans. I went fishing for the snacks; chips, jerky, sandwiches and candy. But I mostly went as an excuse to be with him; to be with my dad. I also remember a lot of time spent with our animals. One year Dad decided we were going to incubate chicken eggs; we put the incubator in my bedroom. Thirty-two baby chicks hatched in my room that year.

I remember Dad leaving for work in the mornings. He was a logger. He loved cutting timber in the Oregon forest;

he was one of few fathers I knew who actually enjoyed what he did for a living. He would tiptoe into my bedroom just before he left and almost instantly I would wake up, but pretend I was still asleep. He would tuck the covers under my shoulders and all the way up to my chin so only my tiny face was peeking out. Then he would kiss my forehead and shut the door again. I would hear the rumble of his old Ford truck warming up while he packed his gear and power saws for work. He would pull the truck out of the carport and coast down our gravel lane. I would open my eyes just to watch his headlights dance across the top of my bedroom ceiling. Then the white lights faded into the early morning darkness. I would fall fast asleep after he left. I hadn't thought of it until now, but this memory of my father leaving me is the most vivid of all.

***

Nicola

…I wish for your sake that I wasn't in here so that you wouldn't be sad. I want to turn your sad into glad by saying I'm doing better in here than out there. What I'm experiencing in here is priceless for me. I will be a better person when I get out. I will know who I am again…

Dad

***

We lived in the country when I was little, in a small town called Marcola, Oregon. I loved our house. It was the last house on Railroad Lane. It was a large gray house with a weeping willow tree in the front yard and an old red barn near the back of the property. The tire swing in the large maple tree was my favorite place.

My parents split up in the summer of 1992. My father slammed my mom against the refrigerator, and she left him. She moved my brother and me into a two bedroom apartment in town. I shared a bed with my mom. I was eight years old. I felt my world had flipped upside down, right on top of me. I wanted my parents to stay together and I couldn't understand why they were apart. I felt punished.

After my parents divorced, my father lived alone in the gray house with three bedrooms and two bathrooms. After my mother, brother and I left, the house was completely empty, only a bed in the master bedroom. No other furniture. My father sold most of the animals and so he had all the property to himself.

There wasn't much to do around our father's house during our weekend visits. My father usually slept most of the day. My brother Garrett and I entertained ourselves and created adventures on the unkempt property. Our favorite game was searching for buried treasure with homemade pirate maps. I was always Captain Hook and Garrett was Smee.

Dad kept his change in a large glass beer pitcher in his saw shop around the back of the house. The shop smelled of gasoline and wood; sawdust was scattered on the floor. One weekend my brother and I decided to have a treasure hunt with my father's coins. We stole the pitcher and buried it near the back of the abandoned chicken coop. We drew a treasure map of the riches; an "X" marked the spot in the back of the coop where the treasures lay.

It wasn't until a few weekends later we re-discovered the money. We were playing around in the overgrown chicken coop once again when we spotted a shiny quarter in the back of the coop and remembered our adventure from before. We uncovered the loot and never told Dad. He never questioned where we found the funds to pay for our smorgasbord of candy that day, he just slept.

In 1994, my father married a woman named Rhonda who already had two children from an earlier marriage. I suddenly had a three-year-old stepbrother and a one-year-old stepsister. I was 10, Garrett was six. Then three years later, when I was 13, my half brother was born. I was never close with my father's other family. I never felt welcome in their home.

***

March 11, 2005 8:10 a.m.

My mother, Dawn, and my stepfather Doug take me to Two Rivers Correctional Facility. The drive to the prison seems long and boring. Train tracks run parallel with the highway for almost 10 miles. The Columbia River flows along the highway too. The river is murky and still.

Doug has been in our lives for the past nine years. He's been more of a father to me then my real dad ever was. Doug was there for the dance recitals, the plays and the swim meets. Doug was there to help me with my homework. Doug checked under the hood of my '91 Honda Accord my freshman year when he and Mom dropped me off at college. Doug handed over the "in case of an emergency" credit card. If it were up to me, Doug would be my dad.

But he isn't.

I have a sick feeling in my stomach. I don't want to see my father. I just want to leave it all inside for no one else to know about. But I have to do this. I have all the questions written down; I know exactly what I want out of this visit with my father: ANSWERS. I'm sick of having a loser father. I'm tired of being ashamed. Didn't he think for a minute that sexually assaulting my stepsister had consequences for my brother and me?

My mom asks me what I might talk about with him.

"I don't know." I say, looking out the window.

"Once you're in there you'll know what to say. He's your dad; conversation should come natural. You both have plenty to talk about," Doug says.

"I think you'll feel a lot better when this is all over." Mom says. "I remember the day you were born. I was sick, so I didn't get to hold you right after birth. The nurse was cleaning your newborn body and you were screaming. Your dad always said you were the loudest baby in that hospital. The nurse handed you over to him in a neatly wrapped bundle. You were still screaming at the top of your little lungs. Then he said your name. 'Nicole.' He started talking to you and suddenly the screaming stopped and the tears disappeared. He says he thinks this happened because he used to talk to you through my belly. You knew the voice in that hospital room was the same voice you'd heard in my womb. Your dad and you have always had a connection, whether each of you has seen it or not."

***

March 11, 2005 9:23 a.m.

We're nearly at the prison. I can't find a place to rest my hands and the orange juice I had an hour ago has gone sour in my stomach. My eyes burn and my head pounds. I wonder what the room will look like. How will I gather the courage to ask my father if he hurt my stepsister? Will he deny it? Was he wrongly convicted? Will we make up for lost time?

I think about the CD back home and what it might say.

I realize I've never had a one-on-one conversation alone with my father before. My brother, Garrett, has always been right there with us, he always cleared the dead air of silence. My father and brother have always been close; joined at the hip, working on some odd job together, going hunting, talking football… anything as long as they were together. When I first tell Garrett I'm going to visit Dad in prison, it surprises him. The first thing he asks is if he can come along.

I tell Garrett he can't come with me, because Garrett is 17 and a minor and Dad had committed a crime against a minor, so Garrett isn't allowed to visit him. Garrett is angry and jealous.

"This isn't fair," Garrett shouts. "Dad never once tried anything with me! He didn't even think about it! Why am I the one being punished? I want to see my dad and he wants to see me. This whole thing is stupid."

"Are you okay?" I ask.

"Tell him 'Hi' for me; tell him that I love him," he says, fiddling with the TV remote.

I can tell Garrett is bothered and jealous he can't come with me. To make him feel better I ask him to help me recall memories about our dad growing up.

"Remember how Dad always walked around the house only in this underwear?" I ask.

"Remember that time you wanted a drink of Dad's Squirt and you took a drink out of his spit bottle instead?" he asks.

"Ugh, yeah, he always wore jeans with a Skoal ring in the back pocket."

"With Budweiser suspenders," my brother adds.

I don't mention the memories I have of Dad missing every dance recital of mine and making every football game of Garrett's. I leave out the part about Dad never helping me with my swim stroke but always showing Garrett what went on under the hood of a truck.

***

Nicola

…I miss you Nicola and I have for a long time. I hope

from the things I have written to you, you can understand how much. I just hope, now that you're older, we can talk about things that are already molded…

Dad

***

March 11, 2005 9:30 a.m.

We arrive at the prison. I walk across the empty visitor's parking lot, leaving Doug and my mom back at the truck. I'm doing this alone. I worry I will not keep my composure. I worry I will not confront him about the crime.

I walk into a red brick building with low vaulted ceilings. There are green holding lockers to my right where I must leave my tape recorder and list of questions. I'm not allowed to bring anything with me, but it's OK because I know what to ask. I pass through a metal detector three different times before the two correctional officers take me over to get my hand stamped. I walk down a hallway to an outside door. I'm held in a retaining cell until the next door opens and I follow a breezeway toward a much larger building that smells of fish. The officer tells me it's Fish Friday.

I'm led into a visiting room with white walls and 10 rows of chairs lined up on the black floor. Couples face each other in some of the chairs. There are makeshift coffee tables made from wooden boxes painted black. Artwork created by prisoners is tacked on the walls. The names of the artists are tagged under each work of art - the drawing of the American flag, the sketch of a lion, the painting of a mountain landscape.

The officer tells me I may hug and kiss my father, but only when I first see him and when I'm about to leave. I can only hold his hand, no other touching is permitted.

He says I may purchase a snack or a soda from the vending machines but I'm not allowed to share them with my father. He says I can buy a separate snack for my father, but once I've handed it to him I can't take it back. He emphasizes again I may not share. I feel guilty I didn't bring any change.

I start crying.

The officer hands me a square of tissue torn off a roll of toilet paper. He says to sit tight and wait for my father. I wait 10 minutes. I want to bolt out of this room and never look back. Then my father enters through the back door of the visitor's dayroom. I break down to another level. I sob.

My father has lost some weight and I can tell he's been working out. He has a well-kept, trimmed beard. I remember that in the summers, he would always have a dark tan, which he attributed to his Indian roots. He would shave his full beard off, to keep cool and he would always slim down. In the winters he would grow the full Grizzly Adams beard back and gain weight in his gut.

I'm surprised to see how old he looks. His hair has been receding since he was in his early 30's, and now it has thinned to a peppered black and white fluff of hair above the forehead and sideburns. Behind his '70's-looking glasses, his dark brown eyes seem foreign. I really don't know this man sitting in front of me. I just know he's my father. He wears dark blue jeans with orange letters 'TRCI' patched on the left thigh and a blue collar shirt, and worn-out brown shoes.

"You're the last person in the world I ever thought I'd see in here," he says.

I can't believe it either. This time the officer brings me the entire roll of toilet paper. My father asks about Garrett. He asks about Mom. I chat. I smile. I cry. But I can't bring myself to ask if he hurt my stepsister.

My father tells me that as a child, he grew up with an alcoholic father and a working mother. He took care of himself. Sure, he always had a warm bed to sleep in at night, a hot meal and Christian discipline, but he never had any emotional support or love. This relationship has happened between us too. I tell the bearded stranger in front of me that I hate seeing him in here. He needs fresh air in his lungs, the breeze on his cheek, wide-open space. He doesn't belong in an isolated prison in Oregon.

Now I have to share the toilet paper roll with my father. We only have 10 minutes left to our visit, I know because I keep looking at the clock above my father's head. I feel sorry for my father. I didn't expect this, but I hope that time will stop just this once and we can stay in this place forever using this time to catch up. But I need to ask him the question that's been burning a hole in my mind since the day I found out. I need to ask him if whatever is recorded on the CD from his sentencing is true.

My throat constricts. Then the guard says visiting hours are over. Dad tells me not to worry about all the little things in my life right now. He tells me to live in the moment and never take life for granted. He tells me to forgive and forget. He tells me to talk to God every day.

I reach across the black box and hug my father. I tell him for the first time in 10 years that I love him. As I line up to leave the room, my father blows me a kiss.

In the breezeway I smell Fish Friday and I know that my father is on his way to eat lunch and I wish I were joining him.

As I make my way across the empty parking lot once again, I notice just how nice of a day it is outside. The light wind is crisp and the sun is warm on my arms and face.

I need the safety of my mother's arms. I melt into her shoulder. We laugh because I've smeared mascara all over her shirt. She tucks my hair behind my ear. I tell her I never asked my father if he is a pedophile.

My mother says she knew I couldn't do it.

"Are you okay?" she asks.

"I wasn't a reporter in there. I couldn't ask my question, I was just his daughter. I don't even know who that man is in there, Mom."

"I know," she says. "I knew when I asked you earlier that it was going to turn out like this, I'm just glad you came all this way to see him. This is good for you."

My father never molested me.

How could he be a pedophile?

***

March 18, 2005 9:51 p.m.

I am back at ASU. I don't talk about my spring break. I still dread listening to the CD from the court. I need to hear my father's confession, but I can't push the play button.

I wonder if he had wanted to abuse me, and that's the reason he stayed away from me when I was little. I need answers still, and the CD is all I have left, since I couldn't bring myself to ask my father anything during our visit. Finally, I ask my roommate to help me out by pushing the play button.

The prosecutor states the facts.

"The victim in this case was the stepdaughter of the defendant… It was reported that on approximately five or six occasions the defendant had the victim rub lotion on his penis and on at least one occasion it was reported that he licked her breasts."

I hear my father's voice.

"Everything written on this paper is true but one

thing," my father tells the judge.

"I have to admit being a sinful, malicious, piece of dirt is not a good thing when you find out that's what you've been. I'm a very sinful man. I've caused a great sin towards my whole family, not just to the family I can't go back to. I have a lot of people in this world who love me. I'm thankful there are some who are able to forgive me... I never once threatened my daughter; I never once terrorized my daughter. There was never any verbal abuse, there never was any physical abuse, and there definitely was sexual abuse."

My father's voice breaks, he sounds remorseful. But then in a roundabout way, he blames my stepsister for what had happened. "She was curious about me," he said, "and I didn't realize what was going on. I never realized my sexual feelings for her until she was seven years old. I treated her as my first daughter Nicole... I helped with her bath, helped her go to the bathroom."

He had fallen in love with my stepsister.

"I never once went against her will," my father tells the judge. "I never once made her do anything. We had a very loving precious relationship... I don't feel good at all about what I've done. I miss my daughter, and I know she misses me... Sexual abuse is nothing I am proud of. It's hard to explain the relationship that we had for a few years."

Then my father feels sorry for himself. "My depression comes to a point where you don't feel anything any more. You just want to die. You want to commit suicide; you want to end your life... You get so wrapped up in your depression. Where it comes from I don't know... When you get depressed you lose your feeling about anything, the only thing that made me feel alive in these depressive states of mind was pain. Why I don't know, I just didn't feel anything else. And it's not in my heart, but in my mind. If I could give my heart out there and show it to everybody in this world, you might be surprised what's really in my heart. I never wanted to hurt anybody. Never."

The judge pronounces the sentence in a monotone.

"You'll be sentenced to 75 months. The post prison supervision is 120 months... You'll be required to submit to DNA testing. You're also going to have to register as a sex offender. That will be for the rest of your life. I recommend that, as conditions of post prison supervision, you have no contact with the victim or her immediate family. I recommend that you have the standard sex offender conditions, no contact with minor females."

***

March 19, 2005 11:20 p.m.

I cannot explain why I still love my distant father, but somehow, under the roof of the medium security prison, I felt as if we finally understood we needed each other as father and daughter. But how do we sustain a normal relationship?

My father's confession to the judge plays over and over in my head. I'd put off listening to the CD because on some level I knew I couldn't have visited him if I'd heard the confession before.

My father did unspeakable things to a defenseless child, and yet I feel I need to be strong and love him for who he is. He has to live the rest of his life knowing what he did was a sin. He'll also have to live the rest of his life knowing that I will never fully trust him, and will never leave him alone with my children when I have them.

***

After the prison visit, I receive another letter. He spells my name right this time.

Nicole

...I am here to help you find truth and understanding. I will never tell you what to believe, that is between you and God alone. I will tell you what is in my heart and how I feel and all I know about my relationship with God. I will give you things to think about but will never tell you what to believe! I love you Nicole Marie. Thank you so much for your letter. Thank you too for coming so far to see me. Love you forever...

Dad

***

I know the answer now.
My father is a pedophile.

everything decided forever

Jennifer La Lima, Hofstra University

Everything seemed like silence, until I heard myself scream. The phone was still off the hook gripped between my hands, my knuckles pressed against the laundry room floor. Kelly had hung up minutes ago on the other end. Kathleen, my best friend, had been killed. Kelly was so sorry to be the first to tell me.

I ran from the phone, practically sliding into the staircase where my mother had stopped short in fear. "They think something happened to Kathleen," I said, feeling nothing but the abrupt and complete halt of time.

Hoping to hear her mother's upbeat voice, I called Kathleen's home phone. It was a detective who answered. I don't even remember breathing as this stranger quickly told me the story that would break my heart forever: Kathleen had been killed by her boyfriend, Tom, at her Columbia University dorm.

The following afternoon, Tom's body was found in pieces after he jumped in front of an uptown subway train. Kathleen's picture ID was in his pocket. "Fear" was spelled out in graffiti on the subway station wall.

This couldn't be happening.

The voices on the news that night had never seemed so strange, as they murmured simple tidbits of a person and a life they knew nothing about: "Kathleen Roskot, 19, was found covered in blood, beaten and stabbed on her dorm room floor…a magazine featuring Jack Kerouac covered her face…Kathleen Roskot was allegedly killed by her boy-friend…Kathleen Roskot, an Ivy League student, mourned here today by family and friends."

Did they know that Jack Kerouac was one of her favorite writers?

Kathleen's name and yearbook photo were everywhere. It was a journalist who first notified Kathleen's parents that something had happened to their daughter. Eager to get a story, a reporter rang their phone to ask how the Roskots felt about the murder of their daughter. Another journalist knocked on their door. To them, it was a story. To the Roskots, it was the beginning of the rest of their lives.

That night, I was in so much disbelief that I called her dorm room.

I got the Rolling Stones: "Pleased to meet you, won't you guess my name?" Her answering machine sang "Sympathy For The Devil," as usual.

"Hey this is Kathleen; I'm not here right now. Leave a message and I'll get back to you, thanks. Bye." I left one. Looking back, I don't know what I was thinking.

I cried the rest of the night in a way that purged the youthful innocence we'd all still held onto from high school. I was unable to comprehend, in the moment, that everything happening around me implied something that was forever. The phone calls. The TV announcing her death, over and over again, like it was the first time every time. I didn't understand the story she was being reduced to, and I certainly didn't understand journalism. I just sat in the dark with the TV light in my eyes, barely seeing, as I watched the video of her covered body being carried away.

I searched through my box of old journals to find the one that Kathleen and I had shared in our senior year of high school. We would write entries together, or read to each other what we had written. Our journals were mostly jumbles of quotes scribbled on post-its, detailed stories of everything that we did that weekend and our latest philosophies on life itself. We loved to read, we loved to write and we loved to tell stories – the same stories – again and again, like they had never lost their original zing. Kathleen told a story like it was the most enthralling thing you'd ever hear. At her funeral, many of her close friends reminisced about her unique, joyful voice, as well as her hysterically contagious laugh.

In the journal, I came across a letter Kathleen had written to me before we began college. The letter began with a Jack Kerouac quote: "It made me think that everything was about to arrive – the moment when you know all and everything is decided forever."

I stopped reading.

Suddenly these words had a new and heartbreaking meaning.

"We may go far," she wrote, "but we'll never forget." The letter overflowed with her words of remembrance and inspiration. She recounted the memories of the Bay Shore childhoods we were about to leave behind, and projected her wishes for the lives that were before us as young adults. She had always had a handful of best girlfriends, to whom she brought unyielding loyalty and esteem. She was the girl who could always entertain herself and all others at any place, any time. She was the girl who could talk lacrosse with the boys, while each of them secretly wondered if they just might be in love with her. She was the spirit that you could feel enter the party before her flip-flops could flip-flap through the door.

That was Kathleen. . .

As the news continued its attempt to answer the unanswerable question of "Why?," Cosmopolitan magazine prepared to cover Kathleen's story in its June 2000 issue.

There is nothing that Cosmopolitan magazine reminds

me of more than picking up Kathleen for the beach. Picking up Kathleen for the beach went the same way every time. I'd drive up to the front of her house knowing she'd be ready and waiting on her front lawn, in the sun. My backseat would be littered with every imaginable beach essential, while Kathleen's preparation consisted of a few things: a water bottle, sometimes a towel, a Cosmopolitan magazine and a big, old book.

In June 2000, I stood in the grocery line and picked up Cosmopolitan. Her photo and story filled pages inside.

For a while after her death, conversations would run through my mind from when Tom, the California wrestler and former Columbia student, returned to New York. Kathleen knew Tom only from her circle of college friends. I remember her telling me about this mysterious, intelligent person whom she had met through her friends. Tom told her within days of meeting her that he thought he could love her. A stranger to Kathleen, Tom immediately connected to her profound feelings about life itself and her love for Kerouac.

Many times, when I would call Kathleen at her dorm, she would put him on the phone so we could get to know each other better. He would often speak to me about California, since I dreamed of living there one day. He would describe it as beautiful, peaceful and wonderfully laid back. When I finally met Tom, he seemed pensive and obviously enamored with Kathleen.

In the days after her death, I fantasized about Kathleen coming to me one day when I was much older. We'd both be married, with small children. She would tell me that she had a very important reason to disappear for some time. She would say she was so sorry she had to leave everyone. Other times, I would just dream about everything I wanted to say to her when we could finally be together again. If there is a heaven, I've prayed enough times to know that she will be the one waiting at the gate to meet me, with her long brown hair and flip-flops. And we will be 19 again.

I've found that when you speak of someone who has passed in such a violent way, you often get a reaction as though you've just spoken about a ghost. This reaction makes my heart sink every time, because it's a reminder that her name is sometimes associated more with fear and the way that she died, than with the life she lived. To me, she is the same unequivocal girl. I can still hear her laughing, with life exuding from the tips of her red painted toes and silver toe rings, to her bright and knowing eyes.

Specialized Business Press Article

gripping reality

Kerrin McNamara, Humber Institute of Technology

Rain made a slushy mess of the Toronto streets leading to Jackman Hall at the Art Gallery of Ontario. Still, a crowd trudged through the drizzle to see Peter Raymont's Shake Hands With the Devil. The documentary was fresh off an award-winning run at the 2005 Sundance film festival.

The theatre hushed the moment the lights turned down and Gen. Roméo Dallaire appeared onscreen, revisiting Rwanda ten years after witnessing the genocide. When the lights came back on, the audience erupted in a standing ovation. A man's emotional victory over his haunting past was a cinematic triumph.

At a post-screening gathering, Raymont admitted between sips of Merlot the success of Shake Hands, and subsequently all documentaries, started with this subject.

"The film is good because he's great. It's not me," he says. "I was just like a witness."

Luck accounts for the poignant scenes, like when Dallaire agrees to visit the memorial with hundreds of skulls. Or when he recounts how the bodies were piled at the morgue.

Without Dallaire, there is no film.

How do you convince people, emotional and vulnerable, to let a camera intrude in the darkest corners of their lives?

Just finding a person can prove to be a challenge. Alex Anderson, a documentary filmmaker and a program director at the School of Image Arts at Ryerson, says access to subjects is key. Although anyone can contact the person they want to film, gaining their trust is another story.

"Say I was going to make a film about young people on the streets of Toronto. I'd go in there looking middle-aged and all concerned and they would resist me. There are some stories young people can get better access to no matter how much experience the older filmmakers have, but you've got to make the access."

Making the connection and getting permission is the first big step, but in a documentary the stories are real. These people may be considered actors but their scene never ends. Creating a lasting relationship with them is what Peter Raymont did with Roméo Dallaire. To do that, he had to take a hands-off approach to directing the film.

"Donald Brittain used to say a documentary director should 'Get a good subject, get a good crew, and get the hell out of the way.' So I did that. I got the best crew in the world. I didn't interfere very much. My main role was being Dallaire's buddy, keeping him going, and maintaining that trust. He wasn't communicating with the cameraman or the soundman. He locked his eyes on me. My job was to keep nurturing that relationship."

Erin Faith Young used this mentality in her first film, Hardwood. It follows the director, the son of a former Harlem Globetrotter, as he examines his family, including his absentee father. The critically acclaimed film grabbed a nomination at the 2005 Academy Awards for Best Short Documentary.

"My role while I was there was to make sure everything was easy and flowing smoothly," she says. "The director doesn't have to think about where the dolly is or if a location is booked. I even remember Hubert (the director) leaving the Vancouver shoot saying it was the best shoot he'd ever had. I felt that way too."

It's strange how the director aims for the emotional in

a documentary. Western culture doesn't handle strong emotion very well. When real emotions are at stake, the director must create a sensitive atmosphere, even if it's not what they're feeling. Anderson came across that on a shoot once.

"I was interviewing a famous historian in Britain named E.P. Thompson. He's a practiced speaker, tells really good stories, and he was talking about World War II and being part of a campaign to support the partisans, people fighting against the Nazis. We were just talking about the period and he must have been thinking of people who had died. All of a sudden he just stops and starts to cry. I'm sitting there thinking, 'Oh great, now what am I going to do?' I realized later we were all so intently listening to him, it was so quiet, and he was talking about something painful while the camera was on him that he just got overwhelmed by the intensity of the moment. It just goes to show you that you don't even have to be talking about anything particularly personal. The camera sometimes acts as an accelerator to truth."

The camera can also be detrimental to gaining personal insight. Anderson has experienced both sides of the documentary filmmaking experience in her career.

"The hardest film I ever had to do was a film about Che Guevara. Nobody wanted to talk about him because they were scared. It was the least satisfying film because I had to convince everyone of my intentions and they always doubted me. They were never truly forthcoming. Everyone was so cagey because I was talking about somebody who'd been misinterpreted so many times. People weren't going to let me do my interpretation. There was nothing I could do about it. I couldn't be nicer. I couldn't be more honest. It was just impossible. Sometimes you come back from shooting and you have no film."

"I heard through contacts about this one person and I went to see them without a camera. I knew if they were in my film their life would be very uncomfortable, so I didn't put them in. I could've insisted. I don't know if they would have said yes. I didn't go there because I already knew I couldn't protect them. It's not worth it if it's going to make their life very difficult. It's my code of ethics. You leave and they have to stay."

But the payoff of trust can be plenty. After weeks of preparation and filming Roméo Dallaire in Rwanda, Peter Raymont used patience and quick-thinking to create one of the most poignant scenes in the film.

"We made a list in Toronto of places we'd do, and with the morgue he kept saying, 'Let's go tomorrow. Let's go in a couple of days.' I figured he didn't want to go. So on the last day he said, 'Let's go to the morgue.' We frantically phoned the hospital and asked if we could come and they said it was okay, so we went. That footage you see is pretty much all we shot. He walked in there, told us what he remembered seeing and he walked away. It's a very powerful moment. One of the strongest things in the film as he walks down that alleyway with the lights, all alone. When he walks away you know, okay, let him go but keep the camera running. Let him go, let him be alone. You just have to be sensitive enough to know when to push and when to pull back. If you get too pushy, the film's over. The trust is lost."

Young says it's a Catch-22; the camera has to stay rolling as long as possible but you can't lose their trust.

"We're not paparazzi. We're not there to shove this camera in their face and get the real raw story. You're not going to get good stuff that way. If they get emotional and walk away, you keep the camera rolling for a bit. If they get upset, you respect their feelings and turn the camera off. You can always start again."

These unscripted moments are so important to a personal documentary. When it's real life, there's no way of knowing what will happen.

"It's luck, it's instincts, it's coincidence and I guess it's having done this for 35 years," Raymont says. "You've got to be good to be lucky."

But Young knew this, even on her first film.

"If you set it up right in your treatment, it just happens. Nothing was forced here. When we put the camera in front of Hubert's mother to tell her story, we didn't say 'Okay, can you cry now?' and 'Can you get emotional about when he left you and how much you love him?' It wasn't like that at all. I think when it's an emotional story that's hard to tell, people are suddenly willing to open up. Your emotions are very vulnerable and it just happens."

She recalls a scene from Hardwood that just "happened."

"Hubert asked his brother to write a poem for the film and he could film him saying it. He hadn't prepared and he didn't write anything until the morning we were going to shoot it. He got up, wrote something down and came to the shoot. We were sitting in a park and just had the camera on him, and he started to read the poem for the very first time out loud. It was incredible. It was this beautiful and expressive poem, and he got very emotional. That's one of the most touching scenes of the movie. It wasn't planned at all. We just wanted him to read something, a poem for his dad. It was amazing. I think it's luck or fate. It's meant to happen. He had to get that off his chest and it happened in just the right way."

Those moments make documentary filmmaking

one of the fastest-growing genres. Since Michael Moore's acclaimed Bowling for Columbine, documentaries have taken off. Just look at the top 10 highest grossing documentaries of all time. Columbine sits at number two, outgrossed only by Moore's own Fahrenheit 9/11. Six of the top 10 were made post-Columbine. Moore set off an unprecedented return of the documentary to the big screen, inspiring young filmmakers to grab their cameras and find a story. It's a movement that excites Anderson.

"We have students who are interested in a documentary career. It's a recipe for an interesting life, if not a completely lucrative one," she laughs. "But I think it's an interesting life, making films about people you find more interesting than yourself."

john bubala

Developing relationships with vendors is 'key to survival'
for this family man and independent restaurateur
Abigail Bains, Northwestern University

"Sleep is overrated," says John Bubala, co-owner, chef, purchasing manager and head dishwasher of Thyme, a French-American restaurant in downtown Chicago.

After a late night hosting a wine-tasting dinner, the exuberant multi-tasker is back in the office bright and early. With so many responsibilities at the restaurant, Bubala usually finds himself catching a few winks between 1 a.m. and 7 a.m., when he rises to take his children to school.

By 8 a.m. Bubala sits in Thyme's basement office, which is tucked behind the extra stores of dried goods and wine, where he surfs the Internet and gnaws on an unlit cigar.

For the first hour of his day, he responds to customer inquiries – the restaurant is a popular location for business meetings and wedding rehearsal dinners – and scans his favorite websites, such as SuperChefBlog.com, ChowHound. com and SauteWednesday.com.

Thursdays are important days in terms of preparing for the weekend, and this one is no exception: Bubala eagerly is awaiting the arrival of Slow Food organic products for that organization's dinner, which will be held at Thyme the following Monday. He plans on testing some menu items over the weekend, but thus far only a few organic turkeys have been delivered.

An hour later the first delivery of the day arrives. Removing the packaging, Bubala sniffs the fish.

"Just like the ocean," says the deliveryman from the Fortune Fish Co. "Just like the ocean," Bubala agrees. The two laugh at some private joke as Bubala sets the fish out to prepare gravlax later that afternoon. A moment later he gingerly climbs the steps to meet another purveyor. "Thursday's check day!" he yells behind him.

"If you don't manage your sales reps, they will ruin your life," he adds.

Bubala, who has purchased from the same vendors for the past seven to 12 years, emphasizes a weekly schedule for payments and deliveries. Over the years he has developed friendly working relationships with his suppliers, so when his produce purveyor is out shopping, the vendor will think of Bubala and occasionally bring samples of new produce for him to try.

"That's the key to survival – the trust and relationships you have with your purveyors," Bubala says. "You want someone who's looking out for you." Without that trust, he says, operators will end up spending all of their time at the office, making sure purveyors are not taking advantage of them. "How much can you do by yourself and still live a normal life?" he asks.

"You have to help your purveyors keep their costs down by ordering smart," he adds. "You have to have their best interest in mind."

That not only fosters goodwill but also may keep prices down, since purveyors often have a range of prices they offer to customers. "If you can save two percent on everything, that really adds up," he notes.

But symbiotic relationships are more than just a financial consideration for Bubala. "Some guys won't pay the extra pennies for the face," he says. "In some instances paying a little more is worth it."

With his wine list in hand, Bubala moves into the room that doubles as storage for liquor and restaurant odds and ends, such as CDs, chairs and lamps. Stooping a little to avoid the low ceiling, he sets aside a few bottles of wine, which the bartender will bring up that evening when the bar is restocked. As Bubala scans the room, he scribbles notes to himself, muttering along the way.

"You talk to yourself a lot in this business because that's your double-check," he says.

He says he imagines all of the chefs he has worked with standing behind him as he goes about his day, making selections, taking tasting notes from them and interpreting those notes in his own way. Bubala attributes his development as a chef to the many great cooks he worked with throughout the years – those who were willing to instruct a man who was more than willing to learn.

Bubala got his start in the restaurant business as a busboy at Willow on Wagner, a neighborhood tavern that was known as the Pink Flamingo during Chicago's Al Capone era. At Michigan State University he studied hotel and restaurant management and helped open Bennigan's restaurants in the area.

After graduating, Bubala moved to Boston, where he worked with Bennigan's, Morton's of Chicago, the Boston Harbor Hotel and, finally, the Four Seasons Hotel, where he met chef Michael Kornick. The two returned to Chicago and opened March 6 in 1993. Bubala was chef de cuisine at the restaurant but always knew that he wanted to have his own place.

"It was a great opportunity to learn how to fix things yourself," he says, speaking of his knowledge of rough plumbing and minor electrical work. "If you don't, you'll forever be paying through the nose," he adds.

Now, as purchasing manager for his own restaurant, which he opened in 1998 with his childhood friend Ben Jennings, that's exactly what Bubala tries to avoid. On a chilly winter morning, Thyme feels only slightly warmer than the street outside.

"You're not just purchasing food; you're purchasing gas, electricity and water," Bubala says. "Purchasing is not only getting the best deal but also managing things you can't control, like the prices of gas and electricity." So rather than heat the entire building for the several hours when he and accountant/translator/"gate keeper" Armie Arguelles are the only people in the building, the two come bundled up and don't turn on unnecessary lights.

Bubala also cuts costs by fixing things on his own. "It's all about labor," he says. "That's the most expensive thing now." Instead of calling for assistance every time something breaks, Bubala has collected spare parts of machinery he can use in a pinch. He gestures toward a backup motor in the corner of another storage room: "I could lose $15,000 one night for a $250 motor," he says. And in his opinion it's better to invest a little cash to avoid a big disaster.

He moves into the dried-goods storage and then the freezer, making notes along the way. Bubala does the majority of his purchasing between the months of May and October – the height of the growing season for most produce. Since the Chicago environment is not conducive to year-round growth, he tries to order fresh foods directly from more temperate climates during the rest of the year.

Sometimes, though, he says, good produce can't be found. That's when it is important to remember that "'frozen' is not a bad word," he says. "Neither is 'canned.'" Out-of-season berries, for example, don't have the same taste as the real deal, Bubala says, so rather than using tarter fruits, he opts to freeze raspberries from his friend's farm and use them all year long.

At noon Rob Royce, Bubala's sales representative from

Edward Don & Co., arrives as usual. The two reminisce about their shared past, from their business relationship at Marche to when their wives were pregnant at the same time, emphasizing again how important relationships are to Bubala and his business.

"John knows that if he's out of something on a Friday night, we'll stick something in a cab or however to get it to him," Royce says before the two get down to business. Bubala requests a few kitchen staples and quickly peruses the company's catalog. He decides to visit Edward Don's outlet store rather than make any impulsive purchases at the moment, and Royce exits as quickly as he entered, like clockwork.

Normally, Bubala would eat his packed lunch now, but today he plans to meet a friend, a former meat purveyor, in Chinatown, so he gets back to work, advising his carpenter as to which locks to buy and raiding the freezer for gravlax ingredients.

"Most purchasers don't taste anything," he says. "How can they? It came in a box. That's the hard thing when you have a separate purchaser from the chef."

For Bubala, his personal connection to the ingredients is of the utmost importance. "I think a lot of people gravitate toward independents because they know the person checking everything in the morning is the person tasting everything at night."

Before he gets underway UPS arrives with several Slow Food packages, none of which contains what Bubala was hoping for. Instead, there are only books, pamphlets and a few tomatoes. He sighs and returns to the basement kitchen to prepare the salmon for next week's menu. Gravlax completed, Bubala grabs a sack of lobster bodies and goes upstairs to the restaurant's open kitchen to prepare lobster stock for the evening.

By 1:45 p.m., about the time he usually would be leaving work to pick up his children from school, he is careening down the highway toward Chinatown, rattling off a 15-item list of wines to a purveyor on his cell phone. After all, there's no point in wasting time in the business day, he says.

Though his friend can't make it to lunch, Bubala enjoys a quick meal of dim sum and heads back to Thyme to catch up with the employees, who filter in over the next few hours. Typically, Bubala spends the afternoon with his children, returning to the restaurant at 5 p.m., in time to eat a staff dinner, his favorite time of the workday, and start cooking.

As he enters the restaurant, set to trade his purchasing-manager's cap for his chef's toque, Bubala readies himself. "We've prepared ourselves as best we can," he says. "Now is when the X factor comes in: the customer."

At A Glance

NAME: John Bubala

AGE: 41

EMPLOYER: self-employed; own two restaurants--Thyme and Thyme Cafe--with childhood friend and partner Ben Jennings

TITLE: owner, chef, purchasing manager

LENGTH OF TENURE: seven years at Thyme

CAREER MILESTONES: being invited to a lunch event by chef Charlie Trotter; meeting chef Freddy Girardet at one of Trotter's lunches

PROFESSIONAL ASPIRATIONS: to have a good, honest legacy through my work and someday own an oyster shack on the dock in Nantucket, Mass.

HOMETOWN: Glenview, Ill.

PERSONAL: married; three kids
FAVORITE PASTIME: playing with my children and perusing my cookbook library

Reprinted with permission from Nation's Restaurant News

apprentice house

Apprentice House is the future of publishing...today. Using state-of-the-art technology and an experiential learning model of education, it publishes books in untraditional ways while teaching tomorrow's future editors and publishers.

Staffed by students, this non-profit activity of the Department of Communication at Loyola College in Maryland is part of an advanced elective course and overseen by the press's Director. When class is not in session, work on book projects is carried forward by a co-curricular organization, The Apprentice House Book Publishing Club, of which the press's Director also serves as Faculty Advisor.

Contributions are welcomed to sustain the press's work and are tax deductible to the fullest extent allowed by the IRS. For more information, see www.apprenticehouse.com.

Student Editors (2005-06)

Jerrell Cameron	Dana Kirkpatrick
Meghan Connolly	Ann Marshall
Katharine Dailey	Joanna Walsh
Kinzee Ellis	Alison Wright
Natalie Joseph	Kevin Zazzali